"TRUE LOVE IS LIKE THE APPARITION OF GHOSTS: EVERYONE TALKS ABOUT IT, BUT FEW HAVE SEEN IT."

– PRINCE OF MARCILLAC, REFLECTION 76, 1678

The Heart Creates "The One"

The Heart Creates "The One"

Tap the Force of Love to Bring your Soulmate into your Surroundings

Shalaka Akana

Copyright © 2018 Shalaka Akana

1st edition: 2012
2nd edition: 2018

All rights reserved. No part of this book may be reproduced or transmitted in any form or by any means, electronic or mechanical, including photocopying, recording, or by any information storage and retrieval system, without written permission from the author, except for the inclusion of brief quotations in a review.

Author's email: author@createtheone.com

Contents

My First Instructions **i**

The Six Tablets **1**

PART ONE: PREPARATION **51**

Environment **53**

Resignation **60**

Keep your desire a secret **63**

Avoid incompatible company **66**

Social fitness **71**

Closure **73**

Disable angry thoughts **80**

Impeccable behavior **86**

PART TWO: CREATION **101**

Cleanliness **105**

Chastity **107**

Conviction **117**

Consciousness **121**

Charity **128**

Beauty **138**

Suggestion **142**

Intuition **149**

Action **155**

Gratitude **164**

<u>Part Three: Courtship</u> **167**

Control your tongue **169**

Hide your eagerness **172**

Protect your creation **176**

Don't boast about having met **183**

Don't give a wrong impression **185**

<u>Part Four: Commitment</u> **195**

Variety **198**

Maintain magnetism **200**

Work together **203**

Avoid arguments **204**

Avoid jealousy **207**

Conscious love **209**

Play **213**

Space **214**

Karezza **216**

Epilogue **227**

Stay in touch

Notes

My First Instructions

Dissolve your egos and help others dissolve theirs, this was the first piece of advice I got on how to find your soulmate. By doing so I would supposedly tap a cosmic energy that was powerful enough and intelligent enough to bring me the right partner. But there was so much more to this mystery that I wasn't being told. Years later, after finding and losing my soulmate several times, I got so frustrated that I decided to throw open a book written by one of the most admired men of all time, Plato. What I was about to discover startled me, and it was just the beginning.

When I first read Plato, the only line that got my attention was: "If we befriend the God of Love and side with him, we will find our other halves, which rarely happens in this world at present." At that time I was sharing my favorite quotes with friends of mine, and in this particular case, immediately after discovering this quote and sending it out, I laid down to meditate, and was surprised at the pleasant feeling beginning to pervade my entire body: it was a feeling of lucidity, and I felt no negativity while in such a state. This experience not only gave me the first clue to the soulmate formula but it also taught me what love actually is: consciousness.

Almost a decade later I decided to revisit Plato, because

even today I believe that to read a good book only once is a felony. In this reading, however, I found what appeared to be a formula for singles, though inverted and shrouded in symbolism: 'The gods refused him the woman because he was soft and hadn't dared to give his life for love yet, but had tried to enter this world of devils without disguising himself as one.' This formula seemed to have given me the fundamentals that I was missing at the time, but there was still more to uncover.

As of 1928, thanks to a manuscript reportedly found in the Vatican archives, we've had access to the soulmate formula of the great initiate Jesus: 'Love your spirit, love your body, and love your real brothers, and then your Heavenly Father will give you his holy spirit, and your Earthly Mother her holy body.' One of the things that Jesus was addressing in this formula was something I had failed to take seriously: exercise. Even so, this shortcoming of mine was evidence of a much deeper problem: I lacked wisdom. After all, most of my friends were exercising. Why wasn't I?

In 1768, Emanuel Swedenborg, the scientist revered by Emerson, Balzac and so many others, wrote a great deal about wisdom and even gave it a special place in his book about love: "The more your wisdom grows, the more you perfect your form; and this form does not receive the love of all mates, but the love of one...and this union is that of conscious love." Conscious love is the only kind of love that can produce true love. Sexual love, being accidental and involuntary, cannot last longer than a few years. And emotional love, being unstable, cannot help but turn to hatred.

Swedenborg said that conscious love, which is received once the inner mind has opened, is the conjunction of charity and faith, and at its core is chastity. It is no coincidence that throughout history these same four elements have continued to appear in relation to attracting true love.

The talented Mozart alluded to these same elements in his last opera The Magic Flute, an opera which is not so much about finding but catching your soulmate:

"The dark night flees from the light of the Sun (i.e., love)!

Soon the generous (i.e., charitable) young man will experience a new life,

soon he will be wholly devoted to our movement.

His mind is daring (i.e., faithful), his heart is chaste,

soon will he be worthy of us."

In the Book of Revelation, John sees the 'New Jerusalem' coming from heaven dressed as a wife to receive the husband. Samael Aun Weor, controversial esoteric author of over 60 books, said "the only people who will live in the New Jerusalem are those who are full of faith, love, chastity and charity, etc." His simple advice for unmarried people was "patience, coexistence, restraint."

The Zohar, the spiritual text that surfaced in the 13th century and that gave birth to Kabbalism, postulated the same four elements, though more subtly: "Happy is the man whose deeds are meritorious and who walks in the true way, so that soul may be joined to soul as at the very beginning…" Real happiness depends on chastity and love. Meritorious deeds and living truth are the same principles as charity and faith. Here are the 'magic four' in the order in

which I present them in the second part of this book:
1. Chastity
2. Faith
3. Love
4. Charity

What confused me, though, was the omission of one or more of these principles by other teachers.

In 1935, Beinsa Douno, the enlightened genius admired by Albert Einstein, was asked when exactly does a person find their soulmate, to which he replied, "When he awakens his mind, learns how to listen to the voice of the divine and stops postponing things." As if by magic, I found my soulmate in a matter of hours after applying this formula. In 1944, nine years after the formula was given, the eminent Gurdjieff explained the mechanism behind this magic as follows: if you are working inwardly, Nature will call upon conscious spirits to bring you everything you need for your work, even a spouse to complement it. To me it seems that once the inner work reaches a certain pitch, a heat is generated and you become attractive to your soulmate, all you need to do is to go find them, and this is done by following your intuition without delay. It is a special type of work that Omraam Mikhael Aivanhov, Beinsa Douno's successor, was referring to when he said, "Concentrate on the light, and your soulmate will come of their own accord, attracted by the light they see shining from you."

Yogananda, the world-renowned mystic also loved by Apple visionary Steve Jobs, gave us a different formula and related it to the expression of perfect love. He recommended this for the 'advanced few', and if you are reading this book, then count yourself as one of them, for the brain of the genius is not only artistic and spiritual but also literary. The indifferent many don't care to read. Here is the formula: "…[Physical marriage practiced in this world] is one means of soul union for liberation after finding the perfect love of God by intense spiritual discipline, sexual sublimation, and meditation." On perfect love, Eliphas Levi, the celebrated sage and secret mentor to princes, said, "We should not seek perfect love in others but in ourselves, asking nobody for it as long as we have not found it, and demanding it the less as we feel ourselves more capable of approaching it." And with regard to Yogananda's formula, it is almost the same as the others, for discipline builds faith, sexual sublimation ensures chastity, and meditation awakens love.

Discipline was also one of the three laws of love in the Hawaiian mysticism of Makua, the beloved Polynesian teacher who shared stages with the Dalai Lama. His laws of love were: be disciplined, feel reverence and love humbly. Discipline is the outer expression of faith; reverence is easily felt when in a state of love; and to love without pride, which suggests giving to those less fortunate, implies charity.

In 1973, Clark Wilkerson, who also studied Hawaiian mysticism, published a book called Soul-Mates. After marrying his soulmate, he wanted the whole world to have the opportunity of doing the same. In his book he says, "If you lock into Universal Harmony with your thinking and living, THEN will the great thing take place…a matching of immortal soulmates…you with your soulmate." The purer your auric colors, the faster your rate of vibration and consequently the more attractive your magnet will be to your soulmate. One of the formulas that Wilkerson published in his book reads: "Seek the spiritual kingdom, perfect the physical, and through this thou can truly find thy soulmate."

Though I did indeed find all these instructions very helpful, they were lacking in certain areas. For example, what do you do if your soulmate lives in a different country? What if your karmic debt is too heavy? What if you lose your soulmate? These are all great questions, though here I will address only one.

All people do have multiple soulmates, though not that many that you should risk losing one. Eliphas Levi, Beinsa Douno and Clark Wilkerson all agreed on this point. Levi wrote, "For a heart worthy of love there is only one person in the world, but the person, this earthly deity, is sometimes revealed in several people like the divinity of heaven, and her incarnations are often more numerous than the avatars of Vishnu. Happy are the believers who never get discouraged and who, in the winters of the heart, await the return of the swallows."

Now if you sincerely apply the simple advice found here in this chapter, what then could possibly derail your best efforts? Well, the thing is, on this planet people are not yet conscious enough to know exactly how to apply these formulas to their own lives, and today life is so complex that simple formulas lack the necessary sophistication demanded of such an environment. For those two reasons I wrote this book, and also to obey the profound inner calling of my own essence, an essence to which we all have access and to which we should all respond if we really want to find the right partner and make our lives a masterpiece.

The Six Tablets

"There are three important moments in life, three extraordinary events: the first is birth; the second, marriage; and the third, death." This was one of the first things said to me by a powerful being in another realm. Let me explain:

I had entered another dimension and found myself somewhere on the Western shores of Europe. I ended up there because of my thirst for knowledge. Otherworldly experiences were not a normal thing for me so I was a little dazzled by my surroundings and by the divine lady who stood before me, who called herself Kamadeva.

After beholding the colorful landscape an impulse urged me to ask this lady what the meaning of life was. She enthusiastically answered, "Live the love!" Her response struck me not because of its meaning but because of the way she said it. Innocence and happiness seemed to radiate from her every movement.

It was not every night that I got to have such mystical conversations so I wanted to take advantage of my situation to ask questions that were troubling me at the time.

The abundance of unhappy marriages confused me a little. I couldn't understand how people could swear love for one another and then fall into such contradictory behavior shortly after. I asked her about this and she said, "Marriages that break are not marriages: they are couplings. The happiness you imagine to exist in a truly loving relationship does exist but only for beings of a high intelligence and a noble heart. So have faith. True love exists. But only where there is intelligence."

In response to these words, sensations of doubt and skepticism spread throughout my body and I couldn't help but respond a little rudely:

"But what about love? Isn't love enough?"

"Love is the left foot. Intelligence is the right foot," she answered. "Both feet are needed to walk."

Her response upset me so I decided to ask her, "But how much intelligence are you talking about? It's only a relationship, it's not rocket science."

"There is something you don't understand," she replied. "All couples may know enough in order to maintain their marriage, but that does not mean that, when the moment calls for it, all husbands or wives remember to put that knowledge into action. A hunch may appear, an idea, but the problem of the moment is only dissolved when that idea is thrown into action."

Her response triggered in me a memory of reading something about the dangers of forgetfulness. But my mind quickly returned to my own concerns.

I wanted to be shown an image of my soulmate so that I could recognise her if I saw her in the street, so I asked Kamadeva to show me, but it was as if she didn't hear me or that she did but something stopped her.

Then something else entered my mind. It was the

memory of a girl I loved, who broke up with me for no apparent reason. I felt an injustice and a yearning to unite with this love. This yearning eventually came out of me in such a way that I cried the word, "Mother!". Kamadeva then vanished and with her disappearance the whole scene changed. Delightful music began to play. Then a series of stone tablets appeared, six in total, dancing around me. I tried to read what was written on them but it was difficult as they were moving quickly.

I then heard the divine lady's voice say, "On these tablets you will find the knowledge you are looking for. You can read them under the condition of a promise."

I paused for a moment. Before making a promise I like to come to a resolution within myself that I am prepared for the responsibility of keeping such a promise.

"What must I do?" I asked.

"Make each tablet your own," she replied.

I understood her reply in the following way: live what is written, investigate it, understand it, so that one day you can teach it to others.

Due to my intense yearning, I felt capable of keeping this promise.

"I'll gladly keep this promise as long as I'm not expected to be too intellectual in my investigations. When I explain things I like to explain them simply, and as briefly as possible," I said.

The tablets then fell to the ground and I hurried over to read what one of them said.

The first tablet read,

'Pray and You Will Find Her.
Feel and You Will Attract Her.
Act Wisely and You Will Keep Her.'

For those of you who do not understand this message, let me elaborate:

Prayers are thrown into space and are caught by the gods, who then throw them back at us in the form of opportunities and ideas. Well, it's not quite like this but I like to imagine it that way.

A prayer is a desire and a desire is a feeling, not a set of words. A prayer is only answered if it contains enough faith, enough feeling. Faith is measured in three ways: its repetition, strength, and duration. The stronger the feeling, the longer its duration, and the more often it is felt, the more effective it will be. That is why a wise man once said that it is by asking over and over again that a prayer is answered. But we shouldn't let these repetitions lead us into becoming all desperate and hopeless. We can be intense in our prayers while remaining calm in life. Actually, calmness aids a quicker response and I personally know of many prayers that have been answered in one day. But it is by increasing our faith that the fastest responses are achieved. The question remains, what is it that strengthens faith? Action, and that is why it has been said, "Faith without works is dead, because it is alone" and "Faith is energy applied to action." It is action that proves the sincerity of a prayer, and action that makes a desire come alive. Doesn't a feeling become stronger the more we shout about it and take action? And aren't we that much more sincere if we're even willing to go without food for it? For a prayer, desire is its beginning, action its completion. In other words, a person only really wants a thing if he is prepared to take action towards it. A desire without action is more like a passing thought. The amount of action-emotion that is needed depends on the thing asked for. If a big thing is asked for, then a great deal of emotion and action need to support it. If all you desire is a loaf of bread, then all that is usually needed is a little hunger and a short walk to the cornerstore. If you desire the clearing of a large debt, then you may need to do something difficult like waking up in the middle of the night and concentrating all your mental forces on demanding that the debt be cleared. I know a man who attracted $40,000 in less than four days by concentrating like this for two hours.

Sincere prayers are always answered but not always in the way we imagine. Most prayers are answered through people, which is one of the reasons why it is so important to associate with the right people. When a prayer for a soulmate is answered, the opportunity will arrive but it may require our own participation. In other words, in order to lead you to your soulmate, a prayer may be answered by giving you an idea or a hunch to go to a particular place.

My mother once heard these words while coming out of a dream: when you demand, you achieve it. Making a strong demand or creating a strong emotion is usually the most efficient way to get a response, but how do we make ourselves feel in such a strong way? If you were to take a cold shower everyday, and during each shower feel, with your whole heart, a yearning for your soulmate, your desire would materialize sooner than you imagine. Why? Because struggle stimulates emotion, and the harder the struggle, the more powerful the prayer.

Ideally, journeying towards your soulmate should be accompanied by at least some form of self-development. One of the reasons for this is that we may have inner obstacles that push away the prayer even if the gods are trying to answer it. Another reason is that in case our prayers are not strong enough, or if prayer does not interest us, self-development itself has enough power to attract the soulmate, because the soulmate is not an accessory but a requirement. In short, to me the most intelligent way to go about praying for a soulmate, is to enter society happily and intuitively, while maintaining a decent level of self-development to ensure that one remains or becomes sexually attractive.

The deepest mysteries of sexual attraction will perhaps remain hidden for all time, at least as far as their esoteric details are concerned. Fortunately, even the common man can know and has a right to know what it is that makes him sexually attractive. It is not a beautiful body nor is it a successful career. These things may attract some women but they do not particularly attract the soulmate. The same goes for women. A pretty face and a shapely body may attract all men but it is love that attracts The One man. A lustful woman, or a woman who spends a lot of time with lustful people, will naturally attract sleazy men. What we feel is what we attract. The more loving or conscious we feel, the more likely we are to attract a soulmate, even if we don't ask for one. Moods are magnets, but actions are also important.

Most people with a high level of social experience know how to act in social situations. Sadly, there are some people who believe that once you find your soulmate, all is well and no risk exists as to losing each other. This may be true for most people but there are some men who are lacking in social skills and this may result in turning a woman off. The word also has power and we must not forget this. Some people say, 'Just be yourself,' and I agree, but for some of us our 'self' is always changing. Today we may feel calm, tomorrow impatient, then proud, then scared. The soul, or consciousness, is the only permanent thing that we have, egos such as fear are always changing. So in order to act correctly, we need to be present and clear, we need to be conscious, aware, not daydreaming. The more conscious we are, the more likely we are to correctly perceive a situation and act accordingly. If we are wrapped up in an ego, our words may not come out the way we want them to. The woman may say one thing, the man may interpret it wrongly and hear something else. Misunderstanding or miscommunication can result in separations so for some of us an effort needs to be made to communicate clearly, elaborating where necessary, and clear communication is much more likely to happen face to face than through a text message. It is not even what is said that poses a threat but what is perceived. I once said to a woman that she should choose her friends wisely, particularly boys, and she thought I had become possessive and jealous. For some of us, false impressions are easy to give. How we feel and how we act should match. Where there are contradictions there are dangers. Sometimes we need to hold back, other times we need the courage to express ourselves. Our intelligence whispers to us, our egos shout, and they can only get the better of us if they catch us off guard, unconscious. The most common behavioral blunders made during courtship are expressing too much interest, appearing jealous, asking for too much too soon, and expressing frustration or anger. We need to stay cool, always. Eliphas Levi, perhaps the most brilliant mind of the nineteenth century, said, "Excessive desire produces repulsion, being demanding attracts rejection."

Finding the soulmate is easy, if we pray hard enough and cooperate. And there are many people who find their soulmates accidentally. The right words, the right actions, are common sense for a lot of people but for others a conscious effort needs to be made in order to act 'real'.

If we want something we need to want it with our hearts and not just our heads. If we don't feel, we need to make ourselves feel. If we want to attract real love, we need to make ourselves feel conscious. If we want to feel conscious, we need to stop feeding the intellect. Love will emerge in the absence of intellectual activity. If we want to prolong our friendships or relationships, we need to act appropriately. Praying, attracting, understanding, all these things are easier when the mind is quiet.

The second tablet that I picked up read, 'EVERYTHING HAS A PRICE.' Some of the more hidden meanings to this tablet took me years to discover. I will start the explanation by telling you an imaginative story I once heard that is probably not far from the truth:

A beautiful woman has gone to sleep and awakes to find herself in a sparkling reality.

She flies up into space and looks for love.

In the cloudy and colorful atmosphere of the planet Venus, she comes across a stunning golden palace from which harps can be heard.

As she approaches the golden gates, a smiling being appears and asks her, "What is your purpose?"

"I am looking for love," she replies, humbly.

"But love is in you and all around you," the being responds.

"I am looking for a man with whom I can grow my love," she replies.

"Then this marketplace may be where you can find one." The happy being then opens the gates and lets her in.

She enters this cosmic marketplace curiously, slowly, unsure of what she would find.

Before long a mysterious man approaches her and says to her, "I know your desire. Come with me."

She follows him to a table and chairs in the building's courtyard.

As they take a seat and relax into the environment, the man seriously but softly asks her, "I can see from your latent fire that you are a half-being. You are in need of your other half."

"Yes," she replies. "Is that you?"

He smiles affectionately, then says, "No, but I may be

able to help. You have come to a place where items are purchased at a price. Inside this golden building, trades are being made that do not suit your situation, which is why you must not enter. Here however we can discuss your situation and draw a quick conclusion."

She nods, hesitantly.

"Do you know that what you seek has a price?" he asks her.

"Yes, everything costs something," she answers.

"Do you know what that price is?"

"No."

"You are a beautiful woman but outer beauty will not earn you the right companion. An inwardly beautiful man will attract a beautiful woman but a beautiful woman will not necessarily attract a great man. It is inner merits that are of value."

"What merits do you mean?"

The man pauses to adopt a serious composure, then says, "The highest price that I will ask you is this: a great deal of love and an absence of dishonesty, hatred and lust."

"I don't think I have that…"

"Very well. Then what do you have to offer?"

"I am a kind person, but I don't think I have as much love as you ask."

"If you do not have, you cannot pay," he says. "I will speak to the Lords of your planet and see to it that a kind man crystallizes for you before the winter solstice."

"Thank you," she replies, mechanically, unsure of what is happening.

When she returns to planet Earth, she finds herself conversing with her brother and impulsively decides to ask him, "What do you think is the price of love?"

"Love!" he replies.

"Yes, a great deal of it apparently. And no lying, no hating and no lusting," she affirms.

Her brother falls silent.

She then says, "But everyone gets someone. I guess that's the mercy of God."

Now I will discuss another aspect of the tablet's message so that you can understand it in a different way:

Work is the price of all things, even people. To receive friends one must work. Work for others and you will be contacted by others. If you don't have a job and don't make yourself useful in some way, your social life will be rather empty because your friends will not feel like contacting you. If you will not do anything then no one will ask you for anything. If on Monday you give a meal to a starving family, on Tuesday a friend may ask you for your company. People act on impulses that come from unknown sources. It is a cosmic law in action. It is the Maker directing the people. The more we work, the more demands are made upon us.

The third tablet read, 'THE ATOMS THAT MAKE OUR WORLD ARE PROJECTIONS OF EMOTIONAL LIGHT.'

We live in a three-dimensional parallel universe but there are other dimensions, other parallel universes, and even scientists have proven their existence. Beyond this world are the fourth, fifth, sixth and seventh dimensions, as well as the dimensions 'below' ours. Dimensions in themselves are not geographically above or below one another, for they occupy the same space, interpenetrating without mixing, but we can understand the concept better if we imagine them as higher or lower, like on the rungs of a ladder.

Hermes, many years ago, said, "As above, so below." If the solid particles above us in the fifth dimension become concentrated enough, dense enough, they will appear in our dimension, the third. Creation comes from above and in our case it comes directly from the emotional world of the fifth dimension, commonly known as the astral world. Dr. Rudolf Steiner, the popular physician endowed with awakened faculties, verified this truth when he said, "The physical world is the product of the astral world." Dr. Arnold Krumm-Heller, one of the other psychic physicians, along the same lines said, "Everything we do is first formed in the astral world and then achieved in the material world." There is also the mental world, which is also fifth-dimensional but exists one rung above the astral, which is why we start to feel a thing if we think about it long and hard enough, because thoughts can make the heart feel, but as mentioned earlier, so can the body's movements. In reality the mind and the body are our main doorways to the heart because most of us have not developed the ability to feel things by sheer will. If a creation concentrates in the mind, the heart will receive it and then changes in the physical world will begin to occur.

Annie Besant, a determined political activist and

theosophist, observed that when the physical atom is taken and broken up, it disappears. It is not that it has disappeared because that would be impossible, the particles that made up the atom have simply returned to the astral world. What this implies is that our physical world is made up of emotional matter.

Yogananda proved scientifically that the essence of creation is light, and he was right, but he did not specify what type of light he was referring to. We are now convinced that it is emotional light that creates this physical world, usually by moving the hearts of the people in it. Emotion puts us in motion. By feeling aggression, we throw aggressive light into the hearts of others and consequently modify their actions. By striking the C note on one piano, the C string of the piano next to it will also vibrate. It is a natural law.

If a man wants his soulmate to contact him, he must feel so positive that his rays reach her, wherever she is, so that she then feels like calling him. If you attracted them by love, you will continue being attractive to them by continuing to feel that same sense of warmth and consciousness, unless of course you go and do something unintelligent.

Your heart, right now is influencing everyone near you and even the people afar. The heart is always shining its light onto our environment, continuously rearranging its forms. Right now you are attracting something. What do you think it is?

Feelings make things magically appear, but that does not mean that feelings create something out of nothing. It is really that our inner state has a mysterious way of attracting people into our lives. According to author of 12 award-winning books Dr. Gregg Braden, a 'field' exists that invisibly connects everyone. By feeling love, the heart's intelligent rays will use this field to seek out the right companion and attract them towards us. That is why I don't recommend using visualization to attract the soulmate. Because you do not know what they look like. Let the inherent intelligence of your love's rays select and attract who you need and not who merely appeals to your sexual desires.

People have this idea that you can get whatever partner you want, regardless of who you are, as long as your belief is strong enough. There are many corrupt men who want an innocent woman. And there are many women who have lists of what they want in a man. These desires and lists are unnecessary because it contradicts a cosmic law, a law inscribed on the fourth tablet as follows: 'WE GET WHAT WE ARE.' This makes sense because everything has a price and if we want an intelligent partner we must be intelligent. By bringing our kind selves into the world, a kind person is brought into our world. We create what we inwardly are.

Women who are tired of attracting sleazy men need to remove from themselves the lust and the vanity that is creating the men around them.

I personally knew a woman who would often complain about men. She said that all men are pigs. At the time she happened to be living with a group of lustful women and it seemed that these housemates of hers were infecting her with their lust, causing her to attract these so-called pigs.

Negative emotions are more contagious than viruses and we should keep this in mind when moving in with other people.

A wise man once joked, "To us dogs, bitches are given." In the animal world you can have sex with whoever you like but in the world of love that is forbidden.

A nerd will naturally attract an intellectual woman. A tramp will naturally attract a player. By reading certain books or eating certain foods, the physical appearance of your creation can change dramatically so all input needs to be carefully considered. By cosmic law you can only marry who you have created. A soulmate relationship obeys laws and does not violate them. If your animal passion motivates you to marry a person that you have not naturally attracted, a person unlike you, you violate the law and then regret is the eventual result.

Man, if you want to marry a strong and innocent woman, be those things inwardly. Woman, if you want a loyal husband, make sure that you develop within yourself the love and the respect necessary for such a creation. By observing ourselves, by breaking down all those unwanted inner details, we refine ourselves and eventually attract who we truly desire.

It should also be noted that food has a great effect on the quality of the soulmate that is created. If we are what we eat, and we get what we are, then we get what we eat. I do not personally believe that we are only what we eat but I do know that the diet has a significant effect on the mind, which then affects the way we feel and attract.

Some time ago, I sought the advice of a health professional and found a man by the name of Ted Warwick. I was referred to him by a friend and it was only much later that I was able to prove some of the things he was saying. The advice he gave me agrees with some of the greatest physicians I have come across so I will include part of our conversation here:

At the end of the day, when there were no more patients in the waiting room, Ted called for me and I entered the consultation room and took a seat. He was a happy-looking older man with that mad scientist look.

"Ted, as you know, I didn't really come for a remedy," I told him. "I came to find out more about health. When I was told that you were one of the best physicians in the area, I had to come."

"My boy," he replied, as he does to any man younger than himself, "health is simple. But we make it complicated."

"It seems that way," I responded.

"It is," he said. "I have seen so many food charts and food pyramids with so many sections and divisions but there are really only three food groups."

"Which ones are they?"

"The proteins, the floscenes and the gocleans."

"What?!" I blurted out, surprised by this unfamiliar terminology.

"Let me explain: the proteins include meat, fish and nuts. The floscenes are grains, legumes and bread. The gocleans are fruit, vegetables and herbs."

"Gocleans? Where do you get that from?"

"My boy, don't fruit, vegetables and herbs go and clean your illnesses away?"

"I guess so."

"They do. If you don't eat them you will get sick."

"Okay, what about the other two?"

"Without floscenes such as grains or bread you will have no energy to flow from one scene to another."

I laughed, shaking my head.

"And proteins give you muscle, which makes you feel like a pro and strong like a teen."

"Okay," I said, smiling. "Can these groups be combined?"

"Well, they can, but not well. The easiest thing to remember is to keep proteins and floscenes separate and to eat floscenes in the morning and proteins from noon. Breakfast should be the lightest meal of the day."

"Okay…"

"You know," he said, with a smirk on his face, "food is great! But organic is best. Organic food, arouses the mood, don't blame the farmer if you find yourself nude."

I laughed.

"And there are other arousing foods. I call them special-foods. There are also feral-foods and special-water."

He paused for me to say something but I kept silent so that he would elaborate.

"Special-foods are unique," he continued. "Some are irreplaceable. They have special properties that tend to nourish more. These are garlic, St John's wort, raw onions, cucumber, honey, avocados, egg yolks, cracked chlorella, baru nuts and crowberries.

"The feral-foods are soy, pork, cooked honey, peanuts, cheap cooking oils, most of the conventional cashew nuts, conventional dairy products, hormone-injected meat, contaminated fish, fluoridated water, white sugar, white flour and factory-foods in general.

"That is a bit about food. But there is also water we need. And we need about 2.5 liters a day of the stuff. Now I tell everyone this: drink bottled spring water but not tap water. Why not tap water? Well, there are cities where the water smells like a swimming pool, it has that much chlorine. And why do we add chlorine? To kill the bad stuff. So what they're telling you is that tap water is dirty and that it is cleaned for drinking. In other words, you're drinking the same crappy water, it's just got less bad stuff in it. That's why I don't recommend water filters or air filters. It is better to get it right in the first place. 'You can't polish a turd.' Air filters push the same bad air out, it's just got less bad stuff in it. Lampe Berger lamps are my only recommendation for dealing with polluted air because it doesn't filter air-bugs, it eats them."

He paused for a moment, then continued:

"Back to water. Everyone should add things to their spring water. Water by itself is not as hydrating as we think. Make your own special-water and drink it throughout the day. Add salt, lemon juice, chlorella, magnesium—Oh! Magnesium! The world is magnesium deficient. Did you know that?"

"No," I replied.

"Well! Perhaps raw foodists have enough magnesium because of all the seeds they eat but in general, everyone should add magnesium to their diet. Even a healthy diet will not give enough magnesium. Zinc and vitamin B12 are the other two common deficiencies, and there are even some celebrities who take B12 shots. Zinc deficiency is more common in men than in women and B12 deficiency is more common in vegetarians than in meat-eaters."

"I'm not taking supplements at the moment," I interrupted. "I haven't heard that many great things about them really."

"My boy, not all supplements are created equal. I have seen natural magnesium chloride to work well as a magnesium supplement. Pine pollen or pumpkin seeds are often a good choice for zinc, but you have to experiment, knowing that not all bodies respond the same way."

"What about vitamin C and calcium?" I asked.

"Every vitamin and mineral outside magnesium, zinc and B12 can be easily obtained from healthy eating," he answered.

Ted then spoke more about the feral foods. He said that most of them disperse the powerful forces of the mind; that white sugar causes tiredness; white flour creates a belly; soy weakens a man's erectile power, as does an excessive handling of the ten euro banknote; and factory-foods usually lack nutrition, or are contaminated with additives such as brain-spinning sweeteners or the mentally scattering red dye derived from crushed beetles. "Factory-foods are great for surprises!" he said. "You never know what you're gonna get." These psychological outcomes remind me of the tragic effect that drugs have on people. Drugs take the glow out of the aura, they feed the negative emotions, they destroy the brain tissues of the mind and they stupefy the soul.

After a brief discussion on drugs, Ted and I began to talk about potatoes. He said that potatoes make a person materialistic. "The one who eats potatoes is constantly stimulated to think," said Steiner. "He can't do anything but think...And the weakest people are those living in regions where almost nothing else is grown but potatoes."

We are what we eat, breathe and think. Food nourishes the body, while feelings nourish the soul.

Ted also gave me a short rhyme which he says is the solution to many common ailments:

"Put a footstool near the pot.

We shouldn't sit but we should squat."

The most interesting rhyme of his in my opinion was the one about the habit of chewing gum after meals. He said that this habit can dispose of remaining food, consequently improving the breath and other conditions:

"To chew gum after meals,

puts digestion on wheels,

bad breath will be lessened,

and the teeth will be strengthened."

Ted also told me about the Nine Cleaners:

Fasting cleans the digestive organs; laughing cleans the inner centers of stagnant energy; massage cleans the body of excess tension; open windows clean the air; steam rooms clean the pores; earthed copper cleans away electromagnetic radiation; chlorella cleans the head; Juniper smoke cleans the energies of the body, the bed and the home; and crying cleans the blood – if you are unemotional, use onions!

Turkish baths, Japanese foot patches, Viome, all of these things can make dramatic changes to the way you feel and to the quality of the soulmate you will attract so keep a receptive mind and experiment for yourself.

The fifth tablet was not a statement but a question: 'Is YOUR LOVE SEXUAL, EMOTIONAL OR CONSCIOUS?'

I never thought to ask myself such a question. To me love had no types. To me all loves were one and the same. But when I took a closer look, it was obvious that not everyone loved in the same way.

No offense to the dreamers but not all love is beautiful: love makes us similar to our object of attachment. When you love a cow, you have to be a bull; when you love a bull, you should be a cow.

In relationships there are three types of love: sexual, emotional, and conscious.

Sexual and emotional loves are the accidental loves that people refer to when they say, 'I fell in love'. 'To love' and to be 'in love' are two different things. The former we do, the latter is done through us. 'To love' is a manifestation of conscious love, and in a true soulmate relationship it is this type of love that needs to be expressed and not one of the other two.

The differentiations of love have gone unnoticed by the majority and this has led to demoniacal actions all in the name of love. By understanding the different types of love we are more able to stop ourselves from the stupid behavior that so many crazy lovers are responsible for. How many passionate lovers justify their criminal behavior in the name of love? To marry out of animal passion and not out of love is to tempt divorce and yet how many couples have fallen into this trap? But let us explore the three types in greater detail.

I think that everyone is familiar with sexual love. A man can fall in love because of a woman's beauty. A woman can fall in love because of a man's charisma or sex appeal. Soulmates are different. They do desire each other sexually but sex is not their only enjoyment because they also enjoy the company of one another, and they enjoy it a lot. Soulmates love one another for who they are, not merely for what they look like. Soulmates are, like all couples, sexually attracted to one another, but it is not the prime motive for their love, so sexual love belongs to a lower kind of relationship and the heart should regard it as a dangerous intruder if happiness is desired. Sexual love is a physical love that depends on physical things, meaning that it could only last a matter of years, Eliphas Levi claiming a maximum of ten. A certain teacher once joked that a man could fall in love with a woman because of the shape of her nose. This is a love born of a material thing. This is much like animal love, which cannot count as real love because it does not relate to real things, real things being permanent rather than perishable. When the shape of her nose has changed, when the peacock's feathers start changing color, when the bird no longer sings as well as he used to, or when the nest does not look so good anymore, the love perishes. Animals do not 'love', they 'suffer' love, which is different. Man can make love but dogs can only make puppies. Sexual love, animal love, is an accident, and overcoming the accidental is part of the inner growth process, a process that soulmates are usually involved in. The philosopher Francis Bacon said, "Marital love creates the human race; social love perfects it, but sexual love contaminates and disgraces it."

Emotional love is often another cause for disgrace. A man can fall in love with a woman because he pities her. A woman can fall in love with a man because she fears him. If you are in love and you feel that the cause of your love was not sexual, then look into your heart and ask yourself whether or not emotional love has won you over. Emotional love can often provoke the opposite, which is hatred.

Many people, in trying to understand their affection with the purpose of substantiating its nobility, ask themselves what they felt when they first met their lover. 'How did you meet?' is a common question but one that is unable to tell us whether or not we should continue a relationship. People think that 'love at first sight' only happens to soulmates. This is not true. Instant attractions that are overwhelming and mutual usually happen between opposites, or couples who do not belong together. There is no reason for a spiritual man to have sex with a woman interested in sports, they just won't get along, at least not in the long run, but this is what happens with the instant lustful chemistry that plagues opposites. Despite the fact that overwhelming sexual attractions rarely exist mutually when soulmates first meet, a certain recognition does. It is said that love begins with a spark of compassion, not passion, and their first encounter can often be proof of this. A man can notice something of himself in a woman and recognise his soulmate in that way. Soulmates are not lust mates and that is the main reason for the lack of sexual heat when they first meet. Absence of lust is one of the characteristics of conscious love, because in order to recognise love one must have first renounced some lust.

Soulmates love one another consciously, intentionally, because they know they should be together. Together they form a team, a team to fight for certain objectives that they share. If you do not know what you want, how will you recognise your soulmate, who wants the same things as you do? Soulmates have an affinity of thoughts and feelings as well as identical preoccupations. If you meet someone and lack these affinities of mind, heart, and will, then only pleasure can come from it, pleasure and not progress. If you can't be best friends, then all you can be is bed-friends.

Accidental loves have no place in high relationships because accidents do not form part of a high existence. Accidental loves usually begin with a hope of happiness and pleasure, a hope that Nature implants for her greedy undertaking of making more babies. When soulmates meet, they may exchange a smile, a warmth, a certain indefinable recognition, but they have only found the object of true love and not the love itself. By revealing their similarities, an effort will be made to spend more time together and to devote themselves to one another, gradually creating the love they had always dreamed of. True love is made, not found. Only conscious love can make it.

The sixth tablet read, 'WRONG SEX CAN KILL THE LIVING, RIGHT SEX CAN RESURRECT THE DEAD.'

Among some hairdressers there is an unwritten rule which advises them to not talk to their clients about politics, religion and sex. I am now about to break one of those rules. Skip to the next section if you're not in the mood for the touchy, delicate and always sensitive subject of sexuality.

In our sex lives what is it that we enjoy most? Is it not to be sexually united with the one we love most? Then why do we give ourselves to a passing passion and end up sleeping with the wrong person? "For fun!" shout the mob. And the disenchanted women would say, "I did it because I thought he loved me." And the Casanovas will always say something like, "Right now I don't have love, so I'll enjoy myself in the meantime."

By sleeping around, those with high standards are only making it more difficult to attract a partner who meets those standards. A womanizer cannot expect to retain the heart of a goddess, and a tramp will always end up repelling the men that truly want to love her.

In the ups and downs of social life, I have had the amusement of conversing with a large number of womanizers and have actually managed to learn a lot about their general condition. One of them had slept with so many women that his presence would put souls to sleep. I was acquainted with some in their teens, others in their twenties, and still more in their fifties and sixties. By making contact with these men at various points in their existence, I was able to find patterns that correlated with what a philosopher said so many years ago: "A bachelor's life is a fine breakfast, a flat lunch and a miserable dinner." The sexual excesses in their youth always gave birth to unexpected illnesses later in life, as well as a warped view of reality, numerous psychological problems, and loneliness too. Giacomo Casanova, after all his pleasures, admits to having become not only horribly miserable but also lonely. We could say that his life, thanks to his education, was so boring that he couldn't help but smother the unbearable boredom of his own existence in a bed of pleasures. The historical account of Don Juan Tenorio tells us that he searched for love by sleeping around but that he died at a young age without ever having found it. These types of men don't know that casual sex often deactivates the heart, making it impossible to feel and to recognise true love. That is why people who engage in casual sex, who take sex lightly, should not expect to find true love, because their heart will not recognise it, even where it is found. Wilt Chamberlain, the talented basketball player, who claimed to have slept with 20,000 women, admitted, much later in life, that having one woman a thousand different times is much more satisfying. A guitarist never gets bored with a good guitar because he can play an infinite variety of quality melodies with it. It is the same with a spouse.

Reports have told us that only one man exceeded Chamberlain in number and that this man, among a copious amount of other misfortunes, fell terribly ill in the latter part of his life. A wise man once said that it takes thirty years for the excesses of youth to fully materialize. But sometimes the pain arrives sooner.

On one occasion, a reformed womanizer, who became a close friend of mine, told me about some of his unique experiences when he was younger. He told me that he hated drugs with a passion, believing that he would never take drugs in his whole life. He said that his weekly rotation of eleven women made him so depressed that he turned to drugs for consolation. Roses on the outside will often produce thorns on the inside. The brightest pleasures of today are eclipsed by what we become in the future.

It is good to remember that throughout history no wise man has ever recommended sleeping around or 'trying before you buy'. Man is made to love one single woman and the woman worthy of respect saves herself for one single man.

Now I will tell you about a much older womanizer, one who had been married for over twenty years.

Charlie was an old man and although he was married, he was not particularly happy about it. He had several girlfriends at the time of tying the knot and by what I know about casual sex, it does not lead to a healthy mental state and no one should make important decisions in such a condition, as he did.

"I had a Spanish one, an American one, one from France," Charlie told me, "and then I decided to marry and left them all."

I wanted to steer the conversation away from such gossip,

so I asked him, "Charlie, do you know what I read recently, that the Buddha said that enlightenment is in a woman's sexual organs."

His face lit up. "Ah!" he exclaimed, "and for a woman there is magic in a man's magic wand. But I'll tell you something: I once met an exotic woman and we did what all couples do. We went out together and she would stay at my place and all that. Now on one morning I went out to do something and when I came back I walked past the bedroom and looked at her through the doorway. She was lying naked on the bed and I swear, her honeypot was glowing! The room was dark, but I could see light shining from her *eilo*! I thought to myself, 'Not even in films have I seen such a thing!' It was like diamonds. And there was nowhere where the light could be coming from. She was real sensual that one, real exotic. She left a mark in my heart that I still wear today. But she could tell I was not going to commit and so she disappeared suddenly without telling me. At the last minute I guessed to where she may have run but when I arrived it was too late."

"Why didn't you marry a girl like that?" I asked him.

"I can't explain it. It just didn't happen. That's life," he replied.

"Do you think that sleeping around has a mysterious power of pushing away true love?"

"Yes," he said, and I was surprised at this response. "There's no room for them. You can't be eating organic food while eating junk food. It just doesn't work. It's either one thing or the other. They won't mix."

Charlie is not the only womanizer to have made the decision to leave who appeared to be his ideal. I have known others. The forces behind these irrational decisions can only be attributed to the forces directing the hearts of men, of which remain largely unknown. Throughout history, poets and mystics have often spoken about certain higher powers directing the lives of men and I have often seen this to be the case myself. My guess is that these higher powers have always managed to outsmart the Casanovas, always keeping the 'glowing orb' far away.

And Charlie is not the only womanizer I have known to have laid claim to finding and even having sex with the right woman. There are others and they have also spoken about how the woman slipped away. My research suggests that this happens because of one or more of the following reasons: the first is that they have sex too soon, the second is that they have the wrong type of sex, resulting in the unexplainable vanishing of the woman. My advice to such men would be to wait until a stronger emotional bond is formed or to consider *soul sex* instead, which I will discuss later.

The most questionable piece of advice I have ever received on the topic of sex came from a wild martial artist who was able to train for extraordinarily long periods of time without resting. If it wasn't for his high achievements, I would not have taken him seriously. He told me that one soulmate for life is not everyone's destiny, that some of us have to pass through certain stages, certain relationships, until reaching the last soulmate.

"Your soulmate is the person you should be with at this very moment," he told me. "Someone else may come afterwards but for now you need to learn from this relationship. The learning that you can get from this person is going to prepare you for things to come, for things you don't know about yet. Don't expect to be with this person forever because that may not be your destiny."

"But can't we learn everything from one single relationship? One woman can offer a great deal, perhaps everything," I said to him.

"You can't generalize like that," he said to me. "If you wait around for the right one then you may be without sex for a very long time. And this is not good for the soul, whose power is sex. But there is one thing you need to know when ending one relationship and starting another: sex is a pact. By uniting ourselves sexually, we unite ourselves psychologically, energetically. By a certain secret law, one year has to pass before we can have sex with someone else."

"What?!" I exclaimed, without being able to contain myself.

"Look, certain cultures agree to a year of mourning after the loss of a relative. The relationship has ended and now a year of abstinent mourning has to pass. Common sense will tell you that it is disrespectful to immediately sleep with someone else after ending a relationship, but most people don't know the process behind it. The sexual energies are solar in nature. The earth, by making one rotation of the sun, renews our sexual energy, thereby preparing it for a new partner. Past sexual imprints are energetically erased by time but the psychological effects remain until worked off."

"Where did you hear about this?"

"I can't say. But you can find out for yourself if you want," he replied. He then paused for a moment, then said, "There is a payment. Nothing is free and if you take it now you will pay later. Sex has the highest price because it comes from the highest place. We can have what we want, anything we want, however harmful it is, and no one is going to stop us. We can ask for our own death if we wish and I'm sure it'll be granted. Prices are paid behind the walls, so to speak. The transaction is made in energies…an unconscious person won't hear anything, won't see anything.

"People want to believe in the spirituality of polygamy. They even give it a spiritual name, 'free love.' But it is with spite as with polygamy, the Universe will see to it that those who engage in such things will be shut out of the real world of true love."

This was the last time we spoke about sex. I later did find proof about what he said and a few people did tell me about the inner changes that they noticed after sex. One girl told me that if she feels lazy at the time of having sex, her sexual partner becomes lazy too. This reminds me of the Exegesis on the Soul, one of the ancient texts found in Egypt, which tells the story of a woman who accumulates toxins every time she has sex with the wrong men. Although I do not know much about the nature of such toxins, I have witnessed many wonderful women, women with such great potential, fall into a life of lust without ever picking themselves back up. These accidents are usually the outcome of an infatuation. Such infatuations give women the illusion that supreme happiness is at hand. 'Sleep with someone, you will be made happier.' This is the promise of lust but lust never keeps its promises.

Love, being the highest, adds pleasure. Lust, being the lowest, aborts pleasure. Is what you have an affection or an infection? Is it all pure or all passion? Do you have reasons to sleep with each other or are you feeding on hopes?

Being taken by an infatuation is like walking into an ice cream store after contemplating the delicious varieties in the window. The sweet taste passes and then you're left with the bill. Women get thrilled about this man, the sweet taste passes and then they are left with papers for divorce. Ladies, know your feelings before you act on them. Sexual passion is an exciting mirage that Nature splashes onto us so that we do more reproducing and forget about love. Nature wants our babies, not our happiness, because she likes to rule over many.

Many men and women want to be with the right companion, they wish for it, but when sexually tempted, they fall. They get so excited that they ignore their intuitions. In the future it may be that you wake up and what appeared so rosy yesterday has only caused heartbreak today. "You had your fun," said the poet. "Now it's time to depart."

Illegitimate sex ends in dissipation. Casual marriages end in disillusion. If it's casual, it's easy, and aren't we all tempted by what is easy!

All the suffering of our souls comes from the distraction of our desires and from our stubbornness in carrying out lies. May our condolences go out to all those men and women who are still suffering from lust's distractions and who have not yet learnt to love.

To those bound by lust, save your body for the right soul. Not for moral or religious reasons but for your own happiness. When you are happy, you will attract love. When you have love, you will be even happier. Good wife, good life. Loyal phallus, royal palace.

Sexual joy is a legitimate right of every man and every woman and comes from the relationship between the divine and itself. The deepest feelings of this joy are present only in chaste sexual athletes, because chastity, being the opposite of the most powerful ego, is the most precious virtue, and enables us to enjoy sex in a pure manner, free of the agitations of lust. Chastity belongs to a higher existence and should only be a goal for those who desire such an existence. That is why I have included a more thorough explanation in the first chapter of Part Two, and left it out of this general introduction. Those who do not find conventional sex satisfying enough will learn about soul sex in the last chapter of Part Four.

When I returned to the material world, I needed to learn more, I needed to act, and so I did.

Years passed and I accumulated much research and enlightening experiences. In the latter part of these experiences, I discovered that I did not know something crucial to my own existence: I did not know my own vocation, I did not know which line of work would suit me best.

To find out what my vocation was, I made a series of strong demands to a higher power and was determined to persevere until the answer arrived.

The answer arrived a day or so after the first petition. It did not arrive in words. I did not even have any dreams relating to it. It was a feeling, an intuition that would remain with me for hours. I felt one thing and I felt it clearly: I must write a book.

My research and experiences are strongly influenced by the great Masters that have appeared throughout history, especially Beinsa Douno because he gave thousands of lectures. I do not place too much importance on the literature of today unless it is substantiated by profound inner experiences and by ancient wisdom.

As the research for this book was coming to an end, I realized that the soulmate topic is concerning people less and less as the world becomes a harder place to live in. The three other topics that concern the people of today are: money, God, and world change. It was upon this realization that I decided to go looking for another revelation…

On an exotic island in southeast Asia I decided to seek out the wisdom of an awakened man, a man who had apparently migrated from Sweden though he told me he was born in the Netherlands. My soulmate was unable to accompany me so I took the trip alone. I was told that he lived somewhere in the busy section of the island's capital. After many inquiries I found his contact number and he did not hesitate to invite me to his home.

When I arrived I walked straight past his house, not knowing where I was. His home was a humble one and not what I expected from such a reputation. Fortunately, he saw me walk by and came out to greet me. He then took me into a sunny room which I think for him was a kind of study room.

"How are you?" he asked me.

"I'm okay. How are you?" I replied.

"Good," he answered. "What is it that you want to know?"

"I wanted to ask you about a couple of things that are concerning humanity at the moment."

"Yes," he said, as he nodded understandingly.

"Humanity is concerned," I continued, "with a few problems at the moment and I do not know the solutions. I thought that perhaps you had some higher knowledge that may help me and my students in the future. Money and world change are the two problems I wanted to know more about myself. They seem to be distracting or inhibiting people from finding true love."

"But first we need love," he responded.

"But there are people who have love. Even I have some love."

"But you are not married," he said. Although I was 'with' my soulmate, we had not gotten married yet. I guess he could tell.

"Why? Should I get married?" I asked, curiously.

"That depends."

"On what?"

"On your reason for getting married."

"Well, I guess two of my reasons would be to feel more motivated in the things that I do, and also to help someone else in their own life."

"Then for you marriage would be convenient."

"Okay. But marriage doesn't work out for everyone. Can you perhaps give me some tips that may prevent me from making the mistakes that others make?"

"Sure," he replied. "What do you know at the moment?"

"I think it's all about treating another person the way you'd like to be treated."

He nodded.

"The quieter my mind is, the easier it is to see the reality of that," I told him.

"It's a great privilege to be with a woman such as yours," he said.

"I know."

"Then let me give you some insights that you may not know about.

"God created woman to put his life into human love. By having such a woman you have a real treasure. But remember that you must be precious to her also. In order to be a good husband, be a real man. To be a real man is to be a fighter, not a coward. A coward talks and does not act, a real man acts and keeps silent. To be a real man is to be virile, not sterile. A man shows his virility by doing deeds of love, not by talking about a love that he is incapable of doing. A real man treats his wife with respect and not oppression. A real man wants his wife to become everything that she wants herself to be, and he is willing to do everything in his power so that her biggest dreams come true.

"An intelligent wife is one who will help you, play with you and be a companion to you. A cowardly husband is one who is always hanging around his wife submissively, and who for her sake contaminates that unique and supreme affection which he owes to God, and as a consequence he neglects the duties he naturally owes to his country, to the state and to his friends. Do not abandon your studies and your business in order to be continually pleasing someone. But do not be so enslaved by your business that you have no time for others. A husband should be the head of the family, a wife the head of the home. In family life, fathers make great workers and mothers great educators. If families were organized like this, our children would grow up with wisdom and love. Imagine what that would do for our future!"

"Yes! A lot," I responded. "Love is the height of wisdom, so I guess if we loved more, we could make wiser decisions..."

"Yes, more love is needed. People are so distracted by the world's things that they forget to respect the many people in their lives. But to love everyone is a big thing. It is better for men like yourself to start by loving what is easy, their wives. Learn to love your wife and then you can learn to love others."

"Don't most husbands already do that?" I asked.

"No. Not by my standards. Let me give you a taste of what I consider to be the true art of loving:

"Love is proven by the strength of the affection and is synthesized in adoration. There are three things inexhaustible in a lover: kindness, grace and refinement. A considerate man with a great soul, this is what women dream of. To feel everything, to guess everything, to anticipate everything; to reproach her without affecting her tenderness; to defuse all pride from a gift; to use ingenuity to double the value of a process; to flatter by actions rather than words; to make oneself understood rather than grasping fiercely; to touch without striking; to caress her by your glances and even by the sound of your voice; to never embarrass; to amuse without offending good taste; to always tickle the heart; to speak to the soul – that is all that women want, and they would abandon all the pleasures of all the nights of Messalina in order to live with a being who would lavish them with those caresses of soul that they are so fond of, and which cost men nothing, if only they had a little consideration. Now perhaps you could tell me how many of the husbands you know love in this way?"

"I know some but I'm not sure," I replied.

"Another mistake that some husbands make is in thinking that all women want 'bad boys', that if you are too nice, she'll walk all over you and lose interest in you. Well! If a man is too nice, or one-sided, there will be problems obviously. Interest is maintained by using opposite forces, one after the other. By using only the affirmative force, the positive force, something will tumble because balance is maintained by standing on two feet and not just one. By using only the denying force, the negative force, the same thing takes place. To be always 'good' is to be sometimes 'bad' because the affirmative force does not belong in all places. Everything has its place, even saying 'no'. The idea of a 'good guy' that many men seem to have is not good at all. Let us take the example of honesty. Some men tell all, but a real man must keep some of his thoughts to himself or else his wife loses her curiosity about him, thereby losing her interest in him. Women tend to do this instinctively. The truth is that a human being is a mysterious and unknown phenomenon. By talking too much and revealing your intimate thoughts you take the mystery out of a woman's love life. To feel wonder and mystery is nourishing for the soul. Don't take this food away from your wife. Don't satisfy her curiosity.

"Another common mistake that husbands make is in displaying an excessive desire. By showing continual uninterrupted interest in a woman, no matter what she does, she gets the impression that she can do anything she wishes without any opposition whatsoever. If your wife began to take lengthy vacations without you, just for the sake of it, would you stay with her or would you help her by opposing her and telling her that such behavior is immoral? Leaving the home, sleeping with another, domestic violence, these are three of the worst things that a spouse can do and couples should not break up without such reasons, provided that a sex life still exists.

"Back to the 'nice guys', I think Theodore Roosevelt was referring to them when he said, 'A chocolate cake has more backbone than him.' But men shouldn't go to the other extreme and be all rough and intolerant. The man famous for marrying 29 different times divorced one of his wives for eating sunflower seeds in bed. This is obviously immoral on his part. We must tolerate each other's weaknesses while trying to help each other remove them. A husband is of great help to his wife by sympathetically pointing out her errors, as it only helps her improve as an individual. When you live with others, you will soon see the bad habits that need correcting.

"It is unnatural to be always occupied with someone, periods of rest are necessary…to be always subordinate and nice is to be false, to be sometimes untruthful. If a ray of sunlight shines on the same person for too long, that person explodes. Intervals are needed. A man must always be prepared to leave before she catches fire. The conclusion that we can come to is this: man must remain a mystery, and secondly, he must not love too much. Bad boys tend to do this instinctively but their coldness eventually pushes the woman away. One of the other things that bad boys do instinctively is they provide a sense of danger. The sense of danger excites a woman's desire. What husbands should do is take the advantages of both the nice guy and the bad boy in order to stand in the middle, balanced."

"That's interesting," I commented. "But don't you think you're asking too much? How can men, I mean most men, pay all this attention to their wives when there is money to be made and bills to think about?"

"For some of us money is easy to come by," he stated, stirringly.

"How do you mean?" I asked.

"Money comes easy to some of us, to those who know."

"Know what?

"How money is made."

"How is it made?"

"By laws."

"What laws are you talking about?"

"Laws of work and causality. Laws of action."

"What do you mean?"

"I'm referring to three particular methods. I will explain them but I won't try to prove them to you, you'll have to do that yourself."

"Okay."

"Firstly, there are some people that can create money by speaking. In the objective world, to speak is to create. Words produce geometric shapes that are made of cosmic matter and that crystallize materially. Any word spoken with clear realization and deep concentration has a materializing value. 'Om Shri Mahalakshmiei Namaha' is one sequence of words that call for money.

"Secondly, there is conscious work. There are four ways to work consciously and each person chooses a way according to their situation:

"If you cannot focus the mind and have no particular desire, strenuous and difficult physical work can be a convenient choice and will tend to attract the things you need but have no money for. If a poor man were to engage in demanding physical exercise everyday he would eventually start attracting the things he was needing. The one who feels the most, gets the most.

"If you cannot focus the mind but you have a particular desire that you wish to achieve, then depriving yourself of comforts, taking cold showers, engaging in difficult physical exercise, waking up early, all these things will make you struggle, work. If during the emotion of your struggle, you make an effort to feel a desire for the thing you want, imagining it, it will eventually materialize. It is up to you to use the stimulation that the hardships provide in order to call upon that wish of yours that you cherish so much, feeling the burning desire as intensely as you can. All these physical sacrifices usually make a person frown. It is up to you, the conscious worker, to use these sacrifices to feel the desire that you want to materialize.

"If you can focus the mind but have no particular desire, or do not know what you need, then concentrating the mind on such things as counting backwards, observing thoughts, or visualizing random objects for prolonged periods of time, would all count as conscious mental work and would eventually attract what you need.

"If you can focus the mind and have a particular desire that you can imagine, you can use visualization to repeatedly arouse the feeling of enjoying the chosen desire. This type of conscious work is predominately mental but avoiding doubt, avoiding contrary actions, also help in the materialization process. The mind is the fastest way to earn money but charity is by far the easiest.

"Charity, or material service, is the third method. Everything in Nature is an eternal giving to receive. The tree that is cared for the most, gives the most fruit. A certain invisible and universal law suggests that you receive in direct proportion to how much you give and that you receive according to what is given. If you want to receive money, which is material, then give a material thing to someone. By giving knowledge you will not receive money but if you give food you may receive a house. Of course, to receive a house you may have to give a great deal of food but that is obvious. The only difficulty in applying this law is in finding the right people to give to.

"For these three methods to work properly, you have to be radiating love, communing with your inner being everyday, observing the laws, and following your heart."

Then a bunch of thoughts about money started to swarm my mind.

He then moved away and began attending to something at the end of the room. I think he was letting me absorb the information. My mind though was no longer thinking about money but more about the problem of living in the city. Cities could be improved if they contained more nature and less noise. If all roads were underground or—

"All that thinking of yours is spending money," he interrupted, jokingly.

I smiled, then said, "I just remembered something about the world: it needs changing."

He didn't respond but instead looked over at the window, as if concerned about something.

"Is it possible to change the world?" I asked.

"What do you mean? The world is always changing, isn't it?" he responded.

"Yeah, but not for the better. Can we change it for the better?"

"Yes, theoretically." He paused, then asked, "Do you know much about light and darkness?"

"A little. I know that the light of the heart is creative. But what are you getting at?"

"I want to tell you that those who feel the light within are, while they feel that light, creating a positive world.

"This world is made by the world above, the Feeling World. If we feel happiness, we shoot out rays of light. Divine beings who live in the Feeling World then gather those rays and direct them into the areas on earth that need it most. When the light arrives, the darkness goes away by itself. That is why Ghandi said, 'Be the change you want to see in the world.' But it would've been more practical if he had have said, 'Feel the love you want to see in the people.' Protests and marches are only effective in changing conditions and ideas, but not really people, and it is the people that are the problem. I guess a march would be world-changing if it united hearts and not just bodies, if the conditions demanded would make people think less and consequently feel happier. More pay, more jobs, more democracy, none of these conditions will necessarily simplify people's lives or make people happier.

"If we cannot improve conditions or give new ideas then we should fight to influence people for the better. The more light that people shine, the less darkness there will be. If a certain number of warm and happy people gathered in one place, they would internally appear as a big ball of light and the dark people and conditions in their immediate environment would either escape or improve, and miraculously so.

"Most people want their country to change before they change. If protestors will not change themselves then the least they could do is unite and feel a burning desire or love for the condition they wish to see. A group of people, by simultaneously feeling the same wish, could topple buildings.

"What appears in the Feeling World will eventually appear in our world. To make physical changes we need to make emotional changes. In addition to improving conditions and understanding, we help the world by feeling love and by influencing others to do the same. New ideas and new conditions can lead to new feelings but it is feelings that make the world."

This marked the end of the more practical part of our conversation.

Occasionally a bachelor will ask me to help him with his love life and I will always suggest that we start by spending a few hours together so that I can properly understand his situation. If there is little chance of him meeting his soulmate in his existing group of friends then I will take him out into the real world and see how he responds to society.

A lonely heart by the name of Craig was curious about what I knew and asked me to be his personal trainer for the day. I agreed and suggested we begin his training in an urban park.

"The first thing is magnetism," I told him. "You have to be attractive or else nothing happens." I then guided him through a series of exercises until he was feeling radiant.

"From now on we may not do any more of these exercises so it is up to you to retain or increase your level of magnetism by simply staying quiet, focused, aware and trying to feel desire at every moment you get," I advised him. "Now it's time for giving."

Then I took him to where some homeless people could be found and encouraged him to buy them some food. After we were done giving food it was time to follow intuition.

"Do you have anywhere you'd particularly like to go right now?" I asked him.

"Yeah. I'd like to go to this particular shopping mall, there's something that I'm looking for," Craig replied.

"Okay, and what do your hunches say? Is this a place you love? Are you sure there's nowhere else you'd like to go?" I said to him, provoking him to question his intention.

Craig thought about it for a moment but he was sure of his decision.

"Okay, let's go!" I said. "Keep your eyes open though. An opportunity can happen anywhere."

As we walked towards our destination, many women crossed our path but, despite my encouragement, Craig insisted that he had spotted no one special yet.

We arrived at the mall and as we walked inside, a mysterious woman slowly passed us while radiating a certain attention towards Craig.

"Did you see that?" Craig asked me.

"Yeah. She's really into you. Go ask her out. I'll wait here," I told him.

Craig then turned around, walked up to her and to my surprise they talked for quite some time. Eventually he approached me and told me that they were going to hang out for a bit and so I decided to go and do my own thing and wait for Craig's call.

After their date, Craig told me that he had never met anyone so attractive, so appropriate for him, in his entire life. These were his results after one day of applying four of the keys in this book. Now it is your turn.

"THERE IS NO OTHER WAY OF BRINGING ABOUT A UNIVERSAL HUMAN BROTHERHOOD THAN BY THE SPREADING OF ESOTERIC KNOWLEDGE IN THE WORLD."

– DR. RUDOLF STEINER, THIRTEENTH LECTURE, MUNICH, 5TH JUNE 1907

PART ONE

Preparation

"A natural law is a sequence of conditions; such a condition being present, such another condition will invariably fellow."

— ANNIE BESANT, A STUDY IN KARMA, 1912

If you don't love yourself, then who will? Your soulmate? Not even. We start the process by building ourselves, that's where we begin. We don't need to be the most outstanding person in our world but we do need to have reached a satisfactory level of development. If you try to meet your soulmate without the preparation then you risk losing them by disappointing them. Your responsibility is to hold fast to the prototype that you are in the heart of another. Harmonize yourself with the ideal that someone else is looking for. If you get too lazy, if you stop maintaining your four bodies, if you even start to neglect your soul, then you'll drift away, far from the harmonious image that you once were, and then how will your soulmate recognize you?

Many people like to entertain the belief that their soulmate will love them for who they are and not for who they appear to be. That is a Utopian concept that belongs to other worlds. On planet Earth, where confusion reigns supreme, and where people are treated as dispensable, dismissing first impressions is a rare trait. We usually judge people. We don't seek to know the truth about that person. People are not psychic or intuitive enough to know whether or not you are their soulmate, so you have to harmonize your image, the way you show up in society, as close as possible to the prototype that lives in them. Otherwise chances increase, immensely, that you will be judged. If you keep working on your image and soul, every single day, then you too will join the ranks of the seductive, the star.

So prepare the way. Old habits don't make a new woman. Shed the past to attract the new. Establish the right conditions so that success can flow unimpeded.

Environment

"We make our buildings and afterwards they make us – they regulate the course of our lives."

— Winston Churchill, Architectural Association, 1924

Before embarking upon this journey of attracting your soulmate, or creating the life of your dreams, look around and ask yourself: is my home helping me or secretly hindering me? In 2017 multimillionaire Grant Cardone said, "The best things in my life have happened to me after I moved." I've lived in seven different countries and can attest to the overwhelming influence of the place in which you sleep. Even if you were to implement everything else in this book to perfection, continuing to live in the wrong house will sabotage everything, and though perfection is not required, there are seven factors that I want you to consider:

1. Your Street Address

Many people would laugh at the following piece of advice but please understand that the only reason I am even bothering to mention it is because, from my experience, this dynamic power has made all the difference — the power of numbers.

Numbers are dynamic things, as are symbols, and they should not be fooled with. Numbers are like portals to corresponding energies. They seem to act as intercessors to foreign intelligences, and that is why on one level people are not as intelligent as numbers.

Numbers have the power to harm or to help. Have you ever wondered why the number 666 has always been associated with evil? Have you ever sought to discover the influence of numbers in your own life? Now is the time to take them into serious consideration.

Years ago I used to focus on avoiding the bad numbers, but as I later discovered, avoiding the bad stuff is not a sound approach to getting the good stuff. It is more effective to seek out success. Focusing on not losing always leads to loss. Now, whenever I have to move to a new house, I intentionally seek out the best number I can.

Here's a list of the five best numbers I think soulmate-seekers should be living at: 1, 3, 7, 19, 22. In my opinion the best street addresses are 22, 499 or any other numbers that add to 22.

Here are three examples I have calculated to the best of my knowledge:

30 Victoria Street = 3

Calle 34 # 65-4 = either 18 or 22

Carrera 32 # 74-125 = 16 or 6 (I lived here and it was terrible)

If you cannot find a 22 address, live elsewhere while you actively search for one of the fortunate five. But keep the search alive. And if you are skeptically wondering why everyone who lives at 22 or 19 is not successful, know that numbers are only influences that we can either work with or against, but they are mighty influences. When in doubt, use your intuition.

2. Black Magic

If you do find a lucky address but one that was built on top of a gravesite, the building may be haunted. I have slept in at least three houses that were subject to the forces of darkness. I was never able to remain pure in these houses. The tenants in the building would often appear miserable, or without strong relationships. A sick black cat would always lurk outside one of them. I would sometimes see grotesque faces upon falling asleep. If you are unsure of whether or not your home is plagued by black magic, try bringing a happy cat into your home and watch its reaction. One way to recognize a positive presence is to notice how much movement there is in the building, for movement is a sign of life. Alternatively, you could try using conjurations to break up these forces but I don't know if they actually work in these cases. It may be better to move.

3. Structure

The most revered structures in the world, the pyramids, the Taj Mahal, Angkor wat, all retain a harmonious resonance and their floor plans are all square. This is no coincidence. The premise is that buildings have a life of their own based on their unchanging structure. I do believe that if we change ourselves enough, our own structure, then the structure of the building is not so important, but sometimes the battle is so fierce that it pays to even have the building in our favor. When observing your own home from the perspective of energies, a floor plan is divided into 9 squares. For the goal of true love, here are the three most important aspects or squares to take into consideration:

1. Southwest represents relationships. This cubicle or zone should have a bedroom.
2. The Center should be unoccupied and empty.
3. The Northeast should be for conscious activity, like meditation, not mundane or mechanical activity like cooking, eating, sleeping, showering.

If your home is magnetically disharmonious, try using formulaic prayers, classical music and incense to correct the disharmonies in the corresponding zones, but do not concern yourself too much. If you would like to understand this science at a deeper level, the only book I can recommend is Vastu by Sherri Silverman. Celebrities praise Marie Diamond.

4. Electromagnetic radiation

Wireless technology is the new evil. The fact that I can use a router or a smart meter to legally microwave my neighbor's heart, without his consent, is indeed shocking. The first radio and cell towers were not that much of a threat to most of us but now many of us are suffering from the more intense effects of Wi-Fi, 4G cell towers and smart meters. If you find a positive street address without the negative forces, the next highest priority is to find a weak Wi-Fi signal.

I first experienced Wi-Fi when I was trying to meditate living in a guesthouse in the Netherlands. Meditation was more difficult then and I didn't understand why. Years later, I moved to Australia only months before smart meters were officially installed. My meditation routine had been successful, until my neighbors got smart meters. Then I continued to experience tension in my face and it became impossible for me to meditate. In Colombia, with an awareness of this technology, I decided to move into an apartment without smart meters and I even turned off the wireless router before going to sleep, but I still woke up the next morning feeling violated. What was it? Well, there was a menacing cell tower on one of the neighboring buildings. So how must we protect ourselves? Well, you could sleep in a silver cocoon or use Bio Dots to protect your body, but I have no personal experience of these. You could also use a sleeping mat or bag laced with silver, or an earthing mat, where you meditate or sleep. But by far the best way is to paint the walls and ceiling with shielding paint. Here is where you can buy such paints:

- http://www.emrshieldingsolutions.com/emf-shielding
- http://www.yshield.com/eu/paints/table-overview

- http://www.slt.co/Products/RFShieldingPaint
- http://www.lessemf.com/paint.html

For other protection:
- http://www.newvoice.net/shop/bioDOT.html

Nowadays I simply choose rooms far from cell towers and weak in Wi-Fi. If you want to be able to measure the fields before moving in, a smartphone can help but the EMFields Acousticom 2 is the most accurate detector I know.

5. Housemates

MJ Demarco made his millions only after moving away from his negative mother. When single I prefer to live by myself or with older people who are more mature. My only specific suggestion in regard to housemates is to try to live with people who are not enslaved by promiscuity or drugs.

6. Cleanliness

Clean your home regularly. My suggestion here is to use natural cleaning products, like essential oils. Eucalyptus oil, for example, is very effective at removing dirt. And Juniper oil is particularly good for cleaning the energy indoors. Avoid moving into homes that are so dirty they are uncleanable.

7. Noise pollution

Meditation, or mental concentration of any kind, is a huge

advantage in any undertaking. Uninterrupted sleep also helps. If you can afford to soundproof your home, do so. Some people put money aside each month for healthcare. My suggestion is that you consider allocating some of your income to soundproofing your bedroom, until interruptions become a thing of the past. I used to wear ear muffs to meditate but now I prefer noise-canceling headphones because they are not so tight.

RESIGNATION

"Resignation, the greatest resignation to your destiny! Only this can make you capable of the sacrifices that duty requires."

— BEETHOVEN, JOURNAL, 1812

The first step in any undertaking is to accept your circumstances by resigning from things like complaint, blame or escapism. Quit complaining or looking for ways out. Instead resign yourself to your present situation. If you're waiting for help, if you're waiting for perfect conditions, for a perfect environment or perfect circumstances, then you haven't yet taken the step of honest resignation.

A friend of mine, who also happened to be a bestselling author and television personality, once told me about a very personal mystical experience of his. He found himself in a place where he didn't want to be. He would rebel and protest. He was upset and he wanted to escape. He told me that things changed for him only after he accepted the fact that he may be in this place forever. This meant that he had to stop all the noise he was making. He had to stop bemoaning his situation. Only then was he ready to learn, and after the learning ready to create in spite of conditions.

Before learning about the soulmate process, ask yourself if you have wholly accepted your imperfect circumstances. Are you resigned to your conditions or are you avoiding them? Are you refusing to work in your environment or are you accepting it and doing your best within it? Are you secretly awaiting the arrival of a perfect escape route? Have you resigned yourself to doing your best in your present situation or are you subtly rebelling? I battled with this step for years. I didn't want to build a routine or get to work on myself until everything was in order. First I wanted the ideal apartment. Then the right group of friends. Then a great accountability partner. Instead I had to resign myself to being a great worker even in my imperfect surroundings. I had to understand that while procrastination waits for perfection, resignation works among imperfection. I had to start telling myself things like:

"Today I will prepare for the future by acting rightly in every passing moment."

Use what you have, don't hope for what is not. Accept your burdens gracefully. And know that the best results can come despite the circumstances. Imagine if you were to drop a perfectly shaped stone into a pond. Look at the ripples that it creates in the water, they are perfect circles. Now pick up an irregularly shaped stone and drop it in the water. The circles created are the same. Taking this simple experiment into consideration, we will conclude that an imperfect person in imperfect conditions can create the same perfect results as can perfection. So start living with the certainty that you can indeed create ideal outcomes, perfect circles, regardless of how ugly and jagged your stone may be.

KEEP YOUR DESIRE A SECRET

"The Prophet said that any one who hides his inmost thought will soon attain to the object of his desire."

— RUMI, THE MATHNAWI, TRANSLATED BY R. NICHOLSON

With the heart a person desires. With the mouth a person speaks. Desires throw opportunities into our future experiences and words create shapes that blend into the matrix of our environment. Now in order for words to create these shapes, force is needed, energy is needed. And where do words get this energy from? "Out of the richness of the heart the mouth speaks," said the Master. Everything we say in words is a portion of the soul's substance. And when something is troubling us, aren't we advised to seek relief by telling someone about the problem? I believe that in these moments a cosmic law is in action, that in speaking about a feeling we weaken its magnetic power.

Now ask yourself these questions: By speaking do we

weaken the heart's emotion? Are people who talk too much less attractive? When you talk about the fact that you desire a soulmate, do people doubt you or wish that you don't succeed? Do their doubts and wishes have a materializing effect on your life?

A bright young girl once said to me, "Don't talk about it before it has happened or else it won't happen. Only talk about it afterwards." Beinsa Douno agreed, saying, "Whatever your desire, keep it to yourself, don't reveal it to others."

Have you ever noticed someone feel a certain hopelessness when they talk about something they want? It's almost as if the person feels that the object is out of reach whenever they talk about it. If you yourself feel a subtle negative emotion whenever you talk about your love interests, you need to stop. No one needs to be reminded about what you desire. Don't tell your friends how much you want to meet your soulmate, or how much you'd love to catch up with that special person again, the one you truly love. Keep your sexual desires and intentions to yourself.

If you are in the habit of talking about your love interests, you may need to make a special effort to frequently remind yourself that talking about your desire to meet The One can secretly stop it from happening. Either way, is it necessary?

I once knew a woman who had been single for ten years. She told me that she would frequently reveal her sexual desires to her best friend. Her main desire was a boyfriend who would stick around. I told her to keep quiet about this desire and within two weeks she had a boyfriend.

One afternoon, I had accidentally made a date with a woman I did not want to see. I wanted her to cancel so I decided to tell everyone about the date. I shouted it from the rooftops, so to speak, and within a few hours she told me that she was going to be late. That was how she gave me reason to cancel and so the date never happened.

I believe that in order for a desire to attract, it needs to stay in the heart and not be drawn into the mouth. Mystery is essential in all works of science.

AVOID INCOMPATIBLE COMPANY

"We must be careful with whom we associate, because we are continually exchanging magnetism with other people through our thoughts, through shaking hands and through looking into the eyes of another person."

— PARAMAHANSA YOGANANDA, INNER CULTURE, JULY 1941

As you will come to know, the thing that attracts your soulmate is your white inner magnetism, and if your white magnetism is diluted by the black magnetism of others, then yours becomes gray, and gray does nothing. Jesus said that he would spit you out if you were lukewarm. Be either hot or cold, for the power of a magnet is in the extremes and not in the middle. And know that many are those who threaten white magnetism. One seer even reported that approximately half of the Western population are carrying around black tails they cannot see — in other words 50% of people are negative!

Here are three ways to protect yourself from the discordant magnetism of others:

1. Use an intermediary, like a personal or virtual assistant, to contact certain people.
2. When you shake hands, do it in such a way that your palms don't connect. "The Western habit of shaking hands is a very bad one, for physical contact is an exchange of both good and bad conditions on the elemental or psychic planes, which can be transferred or taken on by the weaker person," reads The Lord God of Truth Within. "The Chinese do not shake hands, they bow instead, keeping their hands clasped, which prevents the entrance to their body of anything of a psychic character." George Washington knew the value of this precept, as he always tried to avoid shaking hands with people. Today I use the 'bro handshake' instead.
3. To make eye contact impossible, wear mirrored or pitch-black sunglasses. Onnit founder and bestselling author Aubrey Marcus said that a celebrity needs sunglasses for energy protection.

Keep in mind that haircuts and massage also exchange magnetism. Be sensible with the advice in this chapter. Do what is appropriate in each situation. Do your very best not to offend anyone. In my unique case I had to avoid most of my single friends in order to get just one date to go well.

I remember feeling tired and toxic after shaking hands with an alcoholic. I remember being marked after looking into the eyes of a witch. I even remember my relationships falling apart after contacting a relative. These are all memories I haven't forgotten.

I knew of a pure man who moved in with a woman who was regularly having conventional sex with her boyfriend. As the weeks passed, her relationship started to fall apart and her boyfriend would visit less and less. Eventually the woman became suspicious of this new housemate and felt he had indirectly influenced her boyfriend's loss of interest. This is one example of conflicting magnetisms and their effect on an apparently stable relationship.

Here are some practical things to consider when applying this key:

- If you feel you are hindering others, get out of their way, even if it means leaving them. If your life-paths are radically different then it may be that you are hindering each other without you being aware of it.
- Beware of single people who have been single for an unusually long period of time.
- Don't exclude relatives as potential threats to your magnetism.
- Those who spill and those who don't should avoid friendly associations. Yohanan said, "If anyone comes to you and does not bring this teaching, don't receive him into your home, and don't wish him strength; for he who greets him in such a way shares in his negative actions." It seems as though Goethe agreed with this,

saying, "We all have these electric and magnetic forces within us, and like the magnet we radiate an attractive or repulsive force according to the similar or dissimilar things we make contact with."

- Those whose astral or internal schools are in conflict should also avoid contact. This can be likened to a university student who sees no benefit in having friends who are in primary school. Internal schools are hidden places of learning that we connect to depending on our internal activity. It is the so-called 'spiritual groups' that need to be considered here. It can take 7 days for the karmic effect to pass.
- If you happen to see police or negative numbers whenever you are with a particular person, start questioning. This warning takes into account the guidance of physical signs. But don't turn this into a paranoia or a superstition, use your intuition. And with regard to the symbol of police, keep in mind that justice has two faces, karma and dharma, pain and profit.

In short, consider putting an end to certain friendships that are, without them being aware of it, stopping you from entering relationships. "Your friends are your real foes," said Rumi. It is when your lover rejects you for no apparent reason that you should start questioning your associations, or when your lover cannot find time to see you.

Certain social circles can pose a risk. The 'culprits' are usually single people. My experience of this principle was that I had to leave my main circle of friends who were predominantly bachelors! A few weeks after stopping all contact with them, I found myself in a relationship.

When avoiding people, try not to back off or feel aversive, because aversion is negative. Be open but disassociate.

The easiest way to apply this key is solitude. Annie Besant said, "Only in the desert of loneliness rises that Sun in all His glory, for all objects that might cloud His dawning must vanish; only "when half-Gods go," does God arise."

Commitments and friendships are necessary, but choose them carefully, and when chosen, preserve them at all costs.

I want to close this chapter with something that will stir reflection, a passage by the brilliant Eliphas Levi: "Aren't there beings in whose presence one feels less intelligent, less good, sometimes even less honest? Aren't there some people whose vicinity extinguishes all faith and all enthusiasm, who bind you by your weaknesses, who direct you by your evil inclinations, and who make you die slowly to morality? Those are corpses that we mistake for the living; those are vampires that we regard as friends!"

SOCIAL FITNESS

"Whatever a man desires most in his heart, that he will ultimately achieve, but not before he has gained through experience, the knowledge of its proper use."

— THE LORD GOD OF TRUTH WITHIN, CH. 52, 1941

There is a mysterious principle in life that stops us from attaining success prematurely. In the context of soulmates, we may be blocked from finding the right partner because we would only scare them away if we did. I met a married couple who had lived in the same neighborhood for years and even had mutual friends, but against all odds they had never actually met. They only found each other once the man had learnt some valuable lessons from a previous relationship. Only after the right knowledge did he enter the right relationship.

In the spirit of preparation, here is a list of things to

consider to better prepare yourself for the right relationship:
- If you lack social skills or relationship experience, go on lots of dates or meet a bunch of new people until you build up a power that tends to succeed every time. Men who cannot psychologically handle a beautiful woman should date more. Enjoy the process.
- If you feel weak, soft or fragile, take cold showers, provided it is safe to do so.
- If you believe that your soulmate holds dancing in fanatical high regard, learn how to partner dance, e.g. salsa classes.
- If you believe that your soulmate speaks another language, start taking language classes.

If you are already making good impressions on the opposite sex, and your dating skills are sufficient, then you may only need to consider one or two of these adjustments to ensure unimpeded progress.

Beinsa Douno was once asked, 'Where are our soulmates?' He responded by saying that they are hiding from us because they know that if we were to find them, we would put them in a cage and restrict their freedom. If you do have possessive tendencies, start letting go of such thoughts and disassociating yourself with the manipulative attitude in general. You may even want to use the power of suggestion by repeating commands in the early morning like, 'I will give my wife/husband freedom.'

CLOSURE

*"If you want to attract,
make an empty space."*

— ELIPHAS LEVI, THE GREAT SECRET: CH. VII, 1869

A guy named Michael used to date a girl named Kate. He knew that they were not a perfect match but their encounters were so pleasant that he continued to date her. Then in that same time period he came across a girl who had caught his eye before, a girl who radiated something special, a girl who looked like his soulmate. Her name was Sophia. Michael did not hesitate to introduce himself and before she went on her way, she gave him her phone number. A few days passed and all of Michael's attempts at contacting her failed. Some more days passed and they happened to run into each other again, twice! Michael thought that this was too coincidental so he called her again and eventually got through. This time he called her with only one intention: to find out whether or not they had anything in common. It turns out that they did, and in a big way, so the two of them decided to arrange a dinner. The atmosphere of their dinner carried a magical charm, and afterwards Michael knew that Sophia was his soulmate. On one of those nights he had an interesting dream: he dreamt that he was dating the wrong girl and that the right girl, by attempting to enter his life, would bounce off the wrong one. Michael found the meaning of the dream to be obvious: he had to stop dating Kate if he wanted to be with Sophia. This was an agonizing decision for him because he knew that he would be forgoing the delights of Kate. Nevertheless, Michael decided to end the relationship with Kate and it was then that Sophia began to show a real interest in him. 'Letting go' is a common piece of advice and it needs to be applied here.

There is a universal law which says, "Nature desires a void." What this means is that if you want something, make room for it, and Nature will do the work in bringing that thing to you. "Let Nature do it," say the initiates.

To me it seems that the forces of nature are always checking to see that everything is full. Many of us fill our lives with partners that we don't love, entertainments that are cheap, and various other 'fillers', while secretly wishing that something better came along. People, that better thing won't come along because you have enough things. Enjoy your life but don't go replacing your soulmate with cheap imitations.

The Law of the Void, if we can call it that, can also be applied when needing ideas. Empty your mind and the right idea will come.

They come easy those relationships that are not in accordance with the Law of Destiny, and they often serve as decoys, even if you are only dating. The problem is that if you are dating someone who for you is a source of pleasure only, you are less likely to be receptive and open to meeting your soulmate. Many opportunities can slip by. Secondly, if the relationship becomes sexual, it goes against karmic law to just drop who you're with to be with The One as in the story of Michael.

If you feel that for you The One is months away, and that you should not remain alone in the meantime, then propose a short-term non-sexual relationship. If sex does not get involved then the feelings are likely to do the same. These types of relationships, though not real, can nonetheless serve as food for the heart.

Ending a relationship is only one way of making a void, and voids can be made physically and mentally. If you're single and you spend a great deal of time thinking about an attractive celebrity, ask yourself how much room you have in your mind for your soulmate. If you're single and you spend all your time in anti-social pursuits, ask yourself whether you have time for a loving relationship. Is your mind entangled or free? Are your days so occupied with people that there is no room for someone new?

In most cases, applying this principle of Closure is as simple as being single. You're not mentally preoccupied with any particular person so there is room in your mind. You have enough spare time in your days so there is time for a relationship.

Here are a few ideas to create empty spaces that draw objects:

- Do you have any objects that remind you of an old lover? If so, consider getting rid of them.
- Are you friends with someone who wants to be more than friends? If so, politely excuse yourself. And remember, don't hurt anyone's feelings. I once had a girl after me and she would not leave me alone. I tried to tell her to go away but it did not work. So I came to the realization that to make her go away I had to turn her off, I had to make her not like me. I achieved that by verbalizing my most intimate and secret thoughts. She had an idea about me that wasn't true and I needed to say something about myself that would contradict that idea. She actually thought that I was the academic type, which I wasn't. But it took much talking for me to get there. If you do not achieve closure with the wrong person, they have the power to block out others from getting close to you. The desire of the wrong person who wants you is a real force that can stop your soulmate from approaching you intimately.
- Is your mind stuck on someone from the past? If there is a possibility for the two of you to unite, there is hope, but oftentimes the possibility exists only in our heads and we waste our time in hoping for the impossible. If that someone in the past is really for you, then they will show signs of affection when you are magnetic enough. If you fulfill all the laws and still fail to get their attention, you really need to move on. Look to the future where someone even more special is waiting; you have become a warmer and more intelligent person so you can expect

to meet someone even greater than before.
- Celebrities, beware the life of 'too much', for true love needs space. If you have too much, you'll lack true love.
- Is your phone full of messages? I once had 400 text messages in my mobile inbox. I decided to delete all of them. As they were being deleted, three new messages came through, one from a girl who I'd been wanting to hear from and two others that were also unexpected. I don't know if this works with emails but I do know that most of us hold onto a tonne of unnecessary things.
- I used to delete phone numbers from my mobile phone in order to prevent the possibility of contacting women I shouldn't, but this later worked against me quite heavily. I later concluded that it was best to keep the phone numbers of those you enjoy talking to, as these people may prove great friends later in life.
- Are your days noisy? The right idea will not enter a noisy mind and the right person will not enter a noisy day. Don't fill your days with unnecessary things. By cleaning out the unnecessary we attract the necessary.
- Unless your soul needs the sex, do not start a relationship with someone who is not The One. Remember that patience is the first step to love. Of course, if you need the learning and the experience it may be necessary but that is a personal decision that you have to make yourself. I have a story about this: I knew a man who wanted to meet The One while casually sleeping with other women. He sees casual sex as mere pleasure and does not think that it may interfere with his efforts at

finding a wife. This same man was once offered a night of pleasure with a certain girl but rejected the invitation to hang out with his friends. That night, he told me that he met his soulmate. Although it did not work out, as he was violating most of the principles in this book, he did experience the law which acts when someone gives up something inferior for something superior. Cupid saw this man give up an abundance of lustful pleasures with a beautiful woman and consequently rewarded him by introducing him to his soulmate. Guys, don't seek satisfaction outside the woman you love. There are some men who believe that by sleeping around they will eventually find themselves in bed with the right woman. Don Juan Tenorio believed this and died at a young age, without ever having found true love. These seducers believe that by having sex with a woman she will reveal her status as soulmate. This belief may have come from a real truth that was misinterpreted by the Don Juans: by loving her she will reveal herself to you.

- Guys, you don't have to have sex with a woman in order to know her. Do whatever it takes to keep 'other' women out of your mind, out of your home and definitely out of your bed. Yes, there are many wonderful women in the world but in a real life there is room for only one. Many may come and tempt you but do your best to ignore their charms while patiently working at attracting the right one.

- Clean out your home. Get rid of the things you no longer use or need. Even clean out your refrigerator. You can start to feel new in a newer or cleaner environment and, from what we know about feelings, this can result in a more highly charged magnetism. This piece of advice will be more useful later on when you are wanting to become more attractive, more magnetic.

- Lastly, if you can't stop thinking about your ex-lover or some other person, consider the advice that Eliphas Levi gave: "Put a distance between you and the one you love; keep nothing that reminds you of her; even get rid of the clothes she has seen you wearing. Take up tiring work of all sorts, always be busy, and never daydream; work tirelessly during the day so that you sleep soundly at night; look for an ambition or interest to satisfy, and go higher than your love to find one. In this way you will achieve tranquility, if not forgetfulness. What must be avoided at all costs is solitude…"

DISABLE ANGRY THOUGHTS

> *"...if you desire to find mutual love, you need to eliminate thoughts of hatred and put together only those summands that bear the Light of Love within themselves — the feedback you get will surpass all your expectations."*
>
> — ZINOVIA DUSHKOVA, THE CALL OF THE HEART, 2016

In perhaps all books about soulmates, there is a principle which says, "In order to attract love, you have to discard any hatreds." This is actually a true principle and there are many books that elaborate on this idea.

Some teachers give people the impression that they need months of inner work in order to get over the past. I do not believe it has to take months. With the right efforts it can be much quicker. For me it was a matter of minutes. Let me tell you my story:

Some time ago, I noticed that whenever I would call a girl who interested me, she would hang up. It wasn't anything I said, it was a negative emotion that would appear below my level of awareness. This surprised me because at the time I felt reasonably loving, I did not consider myself to have any problems with anger. About 40 seconds into the phone call, she would hang up and I would never speak to her again as she wouldn't answer from then on. The cause of this unexpected effect was a thought of hatred. How did I figure this out? By doing a certain type of mental exercise: I sat down in my room, closed my eyes, and quietly relaxed my body. All was quiet. I used my memory to recall the event. In my mind I visualized myself dialing the number; she answered the call; I then turned my attention to my thoughts; I started observing my thought-patterns that were related to the girl answering the phone; I noticed that after about 40 seconds an image of a certain someone would appear in my mind and then would come an emotion of hatred towards that person. The angry thought caused the angry emotion. I then observed the anger with the intention of letting go of it. I let go of any tension I had and really tried to forgive the person I hated. I tried to realize that it was silly to hate anyone because people don't do bad things intentionally and in my particular case the object of hatred had actually done a lot of good things for me. To make sure that I had detached myself from this hatred I kept bringing up an image of this person in my mind and confronting that person, hugging that person, and forgiving that person. This particular person that my egos of hatred identified with was still alive so to make sure that I was 'mentally healed' I contacted this person with a healthier and more accepting attitude. Well! What happened next? The next time I called a girl I made it past the 40 seconds and we eventually met up. Here is the simple exercise:

First: Relax your body so that muscular tension is not distracting you from concentrating on the exercise. If you stretch your limbs and massage your neck beforehand, conscious relaxation tends to be easier. (approx. 5-10 mins)

Second: Recall, remember or relive the event, vividly bringing to mind the images and, if you can, the sounds and sensations. This step is a kind of visualization in first-person perspective. (approx. 5-10 mins)

Third: Quietly watch your thoughts in response to the event, letting go of any negative emotions that may appear. (approx. 20-50 mins)

Relaxation. Recollection. Inner Observation. Forgiveness is not a separate step in itself but can be included in the third step if need be. We need to let go of what we feel during the visualization process. If we do not let go, we remain identified with the negativity.

Now many men criticize women for their illogical behavior during courtship and so on. What men need to understand is that women respond more to the invisible than the visible. Eliphas Levi said, "Women cherish a great soul in the same way that men love beauty." And Victor Hugo said, "Men have sight, women have insight." If men knew the secret causes of a woman's behavior, they would realize that the woman is not to blame and that the causes are within themselves.

Some people think that actions and words do everything. But feelings also 'do'.

The mechanism behind feelings is complex but I'll attempt to explain one aspect of it:

Hatred is the opposite to love. Now if you feel love you attract love. But if you are feeling love and then all of a sudden think a powerful thought of hatred, your power of attraction diminishes greatly. In some cases the magnetism can be totally lost in that moment. It is like an electrical short circuit. Let us take an example: I feel a bit loving but not as much as I felt as a child. I'll give myself a rating out of +10 and say +4. Now if a hatred of -8 enters even only for an instant, my power of attraction stands at -4. So I am in the negative. This means that I have to build up my love all over again if I want to effortlessly attract a soulmate.

Observe your inner world in response to anyone or anything you may resent. A single thought of hatred towards your mother or your father can short-circuit a wonderful connection.

Observe any resistance you may have to meeting your soulmate. Vividly visualize yourself meeting The One and try to notice if you have any internal resistances to it. If so, shine the light of your awareness onto the darkness and it will go away by itself. Let go of these internal things.

Look into yourself and see if there are secret thoughts that are preventing you from loving, accepting, or being open. Do the mental exercise as often as you like – add it to your inner work. I actually find it quite enjoyable, like hunting for treasure. And beware of criticizing, hating and working a job you hate. Where possible, pursue your vocation instead.

Now a word on the secret power of judgment:

The ancient teaching, 'Don't judge, so that you are not judged,' is well-known but most people are not in the habit of applying it correctly. The teaching refers to criticism. If you see a man who obviously married the wrong woman, don't let your heart criticize him. Instead, wish him guidance, so that he does not repeat the same mistake in the future. I know a woman who criticized her mother for not letting go of a physically abusive relationship. This same woman, years later, was surprised to find her very own self being violently abused, and even choosing to stay in the relationship. A friend of mine once criticized his father for his alcohol and drug abuse. Years later, this friend of mine started abusing these same substances himself. I once criticized my friend because he got his car damaged for mishandling an easy situation. A few weeks later, a man damaged my fence after I dealt with him inappropriately. So beware of criticizing anyone for anything, or you may become the dupe yourself. This is the power of heart-criticism. Don't be the hater.

If criticism and hatred have taunted your mind in the past, deepen your understanding of forgiveness by beginning the ancient practice of forgiving someone 70 times a day for seven days in a row. Alternatively, Howard Wills has some powerful prayers on forgiveness he offers for free on his website. His are to be repeated 3-5 times a day. Both approaches have their place and both have given me results. And lastly, if you steal need to heal your mind from the past, resort to breath control, a science that can heal the mind by balancing the inner world. Refer to Sivananda or Beinsa Douno for more information on this practice.

> The cosmos has a number of angels,
> and a place for karmic dealings.
> There is an angel who watches your actions,
> and there are six who watch your feelings.

IMPECCABLE BEHAVIOR

"The whole journey from the Kingdom of Strife to the Kingdom of Love resolves itself into a process which may be summed up in the following words: the regulation and purification of conduct."

— JAMES ALLEN, ALL THESE THINGS ADDED, 1903

It is unquestionable that good behavior is indeed part of the soulmate process, but this principle does not apply to everyone in the same way. Not everyone is expected to behave well because not everyone is conscious enough to do so. The more conscious you are, the more responsibility you have. We are all at different levels of being. A child cannot be reprimanded for licking ice cream off the ground but imagine if the pope did such a thing!

People who have absorbed a great amount of knowledge and attained a high degree of consciousness need to know that depending on the act committed or omitted, they can attract or push away their soulmate, unknowingly. It is therefore of immense importance to neither break laws nor neglect obligations, however small those laws or obligations may appear.

This chapter is more about karmic actions than it is about anything else, but keep in mind that we incur a karmic debt not only for the wrong that was done but also for the good that was not done when we could have done it and for the things that we did that were unnecessary. No angel can smite us for doing what was necessary but oftentimes no excuse can protect us for doing what was completely unnecessary.

Now let me briefly share with you one of my experiences with this law and how it relates to the soulmate:

Tempted by money some years ago, I made an illegal dealing with a certain man I knew. He gave me thousands of dollars for helping him and I thought nothing of it. As time passed, I noticed that I had remained single for an unusually long period of time, despite the many opportunities. Some girls desired me immensely though for some reason an obstacle would always arise. To me it was all coincidences until the coincidences became too much. Almost a year passed and nothing. Not even a kiss. And it wasn't me. It was something else. Upon realizing the strange events that would arise to stop a woman from getting close to me, I started weeding out all possible causes. I eventually came to the conclusion that it was this pact that I had made a long time ago. So I exited the pact, causing great frustration in my associate. A few days later I found myself in an intimate relationship.

If we know our soulmate to be a gift then we will soon realize that we have to stop doing bad things or Santa won't deliver. There is an ancient legend in which Jupiter says something along the following lines: "You have kept all my commandments. Now I can see that you love me. I thank you dearly. Here are some gifts from me to you."

Regardless of what we believe in, the wisest authors in history have all encouraged goodness. A good partner is created by a good person, not by one who cheats and steals. Unfortunately, breaking the law is very common nowadays and some people will even mock you if you choose to do the right thing.

For spiritual people, obeying the law is an essential key in entering a real relationship. For those with other goals, it is not so necessary. In any case, I know that I need to elaborate on what is karmic, i.e. negative actions, so that you can better navigate your life. Though before we get to the list, I should mention that a series of financial misfortunes can also be caused by not complying with some of the following laws. Now here are my extremely scrupulous guidelines, in no particular order, on how we can all avoid adding to our karmic debt. Though keep in mind that you don't have to comply with every single one of them to harmonize yourself with the soulmate process:

- Be punctual to the second or arrive early.
- Pay your unpaid bills and your taxes.
- Avoid gambling, the lottery, and the stock market. To invest in a company in order to support it is one thing,

to buy and sell with the purpose of making millions is another.
- I once got karma for accidentally using licensed material on a website. Honor all laws online. If necessary read the terms and conditions. Many people are using software they have not paid for. Pay for your music and movies. Avoid using the Internet to download content that you have not paid for. Use YouTube and the Internet responsibly.
- Don't pick up money off the ground unless it is yours, for this is seen as theft by the higher powers. I once lost some money and there was only one place where I could have dropped it. I went back to that place and behold, the money was gone!
- If your kitchen stove suffers gas leaks, replace it with electric. Actually, to err on the safe side, always choose electric over gas, or solar cooking like SolSource. I know a few people in poor countries whose gas stoves suffer leaks. Some people would rather poison themselves than spend the money.
- Don't take from the garbage. One of my housemates once threw a table of mine out onto the street accidentally and before I got a chance to reclaim it someone took it, thinking it was garbage. This really upset me but it actually happened days after I stole from the garbage myself.
- If you are a teacher, try not to reveal secrets in a mundane way, or else they will not be taken seriously by those who receive it.

- Pay any and all financial debts you may have to your friends, parents, governments, etc.
- Spiritual aspirants have been advised to not live with the opposite sex unless they are in a relationship with them or related to them.
- Couchsurfing is a useful tool but is unfortunately being used by many as a dating service. Using it to shelter people in a home that is not your own may be karmic.
- If you don't need your Couchsurfing, Dropbox, Instagram and Facebook accounts, deactivate them. Disable unused Soundcloud, Canva, Twitter, Prezi, Mega.nz accounts. Delete unwatched videos or content to free up space on YouTube, Google Drive.
- Not showing enough gratitude brings suffering
- Avoid indoor cinemas and nightclubs. Cinemas are containers of negative thoughts and emotions. In this respect, outdoor cinemas are harmless because there is nothing to contain the negative reactions of the audience. On nightclubs, Beinsa Douno said, "In every nightclub there live such evil spirits which exercise great influence upon your souls."
- Don't steal Wi-Fi. One of my neighbors once gave me his username and password so that I could use his Wi-Fi, but in the terms, it clearly states that this is not allowed. Always use your own Wi-Fi that you are paying for.
- You can get karma for interfering with the karma of another. Disrupting someone else's sexual relationship, even if it is a painful one, is one example of karmic interference.

- Don't rush. Rushing activates fear and defeats serenity, a virtue that is always tested on the spiritual path. To emphasize this point, here is a poem I wrote:

  By rushing through the city streets and jaywalking all the while,
  I upset the gods in such a way they killed my soulmate's smile;
  but the rushing worked, I caught the tram and arrived at my lover's place,
  but all I found was a broken bond and some tears running down her face.
  The relationship was tragically over before it had come to its final fruition,
  all because rushing and jaywalking were left out of my karmic tuition.
  If good behavior was really as simple as the famous ten commandments,
  I'd have that thing called love by now, the highest of all enchantments.

- Don't get into unethical dealings with relatives. It might seem like you are doing someone a favor but you may be breaking a higher law.
- Don't gossip. To gossip means to talk about others for the sake of it, without a good reason. The wise Kout Humi said, "Gossip distances us from esotericism and the gods."
- Don't overcharge for any of your possessions. This is an act of greed. I once charged a couple $260 a week for a rental property of mine and a few weeks later I had no funds in my account. What I realized was that I was charging $10 more than it was worth and consequently money was being mysteriously withheld from me until I corrected my error.
- Give ten percent of your income to a person or organization who gives you new ideas and inner

strength, or to bringers of truth and justice. This is known biblically as tithing. If you borrow money, you may also have to tithe. Here is a poem about this principle:

Those who don't give to charity seriously,
start losing their things mysteriously.
If you start to reap what you have not sown,
you will come to lose your mobile phone.

- Don't tell lies. In ancient literature, lying is a crime against the aspect that guides us. However, there are moments where lying is allowed. Here is a simple example: you are at work and your boss does not want to be disturbed. If someone calls in, you are told to tell them that the boss is out. If you lie, you keep your job. If you tell the truth, you lose your job. To not lie in these moments is to be a fanatic. If someone asks you a question that you don't want to answer, bring to mind the following advice that Eliphas Levi gave: "The art of keeping silent is the art of hiding the truth without lying."
- Never overstay a Visa. I know that many people do this but many are those who fail in finding true love.
- Don't sleep with the crown of your head facing the north.
- Eat between sunrise and sunset but not after sunset. The two big meals of the day should be at noon and just before the sun sets.
- Make sure your home is clean and orderly. This is critical.

- The moment the sun sets, it is harmless to go to sleep, but be sure to wake up before it rises. According to Sivananda, sleeping in the daytime develops gastritis, dyspepsia, and a host of other ailments. Beinsa Douno said that sleeping in the daytime collects the black rays of the sun, leaving a person feeling indisposed. And Jesus said that if you sleep while the sun is in the sky the angels will leave you. The air elementals consider a thing to be valuable only when it possesses the impregnation of the sun's atoms.
- Putting your bare feet or palms on the soil at night is extremely harmful. Always wear insulated footwear at night, otherwise you will be left without magnetism because you're devitalizing yourself.
- It is karmic to take the possessions of a shared household. Unless a clear agreement is made, the possessions you leave behind become theirs, and no longer yours.
- Replace hallucinogenic plants like marijuana, hallucinogenic mushrooms and synaptolepis kirkii with things like maca powder or coffee. If you are addicted to marijuana, consider taking a full dose of Iboga rootbark as it may be your only hope to cure the addiction. "[Ganja is] an evil habit of the worst kind," said Sivananda. Peyote and traditional ayahuasca are not hallucinogenic plants.
- You can get karma for not helping when you could have helped. Personally, I like to help only when asked. If I notice someone who needs my help, I don't help unless they ask.

- Television and YouTube can be quite harmful. It can make the mind too lazy to meditate. Yogananda said that television has a satanic influence.
- My experience of Hatha Yoga is a series of very unnatural and even awkward postures. As it turns out, certain esoteric authors, whose wisdom far transcends my own, openly discourage it. Leadbeater said, "It is possible, by the methods of Hatha Yoga, for example for the ego to re-establish direct control over portions of the sympathetic system: to do so, however, is obviously not a step forward, but a step backward, in evolution." Samael Aun Weor wrote, "I was invited to a great assembly of the venerable Great White Lodge where, right in the middle of the whole assembly, Hatha Yoga was labeled as authentic Black Magic." When I compare Hatha Yoga to the Tibetan Rites, which are so natural that even children and animals do them instinctively, I wonder how on earth Hatha Yoga became so popular. Fortunately, the natural postures of Vinyasa Yoga are developing more of a following.
- I once got karma for buying back the laptop from my mum that I had sold to her a few months earlier. She actually needed the laptop but sold it back to me regardless.
- If you refuse to go to a steam room on a regular basis, you will eventually start emitting discordant vibrations. It is like refusing to go to the toilet or not wanting to take a shower. You will go on accumulating substances that need to be discharged. I suggest people go twice

a week or every 12 days at the least. Take salted water with you and take a cold shower before leaving the heat.
- Try not to wear clothes used by someone else or sleep on a used mattress or bed sheets. The clothes that you wear should have been used only by you. The mattress and bed linen you use should have been used only by you. A transference of conflicting energies can result by wearing fabrics used by others. Beinsa Douno said that this is one of the secret causes of suffering in a lot of people. If you want to get rid of clothes you no longer wear, instead of donating them, burn them.
- I once got karma for teaching certain things in a public setting, not knowing that I did not fulfill the requirements for such a responsibility.
- Refusing to fast on a monthly or weekly basis may put you in a karmic position but this is something I will elaborate on in the second part of the book.
- People can get karma for hurting plants or animals unnecessarily. Pay particular attention to the Aloe plant. And know that if the gel is taken internally, it should only be taken in tiny amounts, as the gel is made of ultra rays of the sun.
- Avoid isolated compounds, aka pharmakeia. Throughout the world, everywhere I look I see children and adults, healthy people, even knowledgeable people, all taking drugs. At 14 years old I knew intuitively that taking drugs would damage my spiritual potential so I intentionally avoided them, or so I thought. Unfortunately, it took another 17 years before I was to discover what drugs

actually were...Years ago, after running out of a zinc supplement that I was taking, I went searching for a replacement. I found one manufactured by a different company and start taking it. Immediately afterwards I noticed that I could no longer feed my soul through meditation. In other words, my meditation stopped working. I then experimented with substances kirkii and Iboga TA. With kirkii I felt a destructive storm rage against my mind and with Iboga TA I noticed how much more enslaved I became to my ego of compulsion. Kirkii is a hallucinogenic plant from Africa. Iboga TA is a collection of isolated compounds. Online information convinced me that they were harmless, that they may even give me a psychological advantage in life, but I was wrong. I then returned to Australia and started taking DIM to remove estrogen from my body. After taking it for two weeks I noticed that my ego of compulsion started becoming stronger again. What I observed after taking Iboga TA I had observed after taking DIM. Again, I had been misled. I thought I was detoxing but instead I was hurting my psychology and consequently my soul... This experience of mine led me to the following startling conclusion: any compound toxically removed from its natural source is indeed a drug, and these compounds are everywhere. Coca leaves and coffee beans are harmless in themselves but if poisons are used to extract their predominant compounds we get cocaine and caffeine, which are both white powders. Most people know that cocaine and heroine are dangerous drugs but these same people are consuming drugs in the gum they chew, in the sodas they drink, even in certain so-called health supplements. This may be why most people are so confused, why they find meditation impossible, and perhaps more strangely, why they act as though all is well when it really isn't...To not frustrate the soulmate process and not do yourself further damage, here is a list of common substances that you really need to avoid:

- Morphine
- Amphetamine
- Caffeine
- Quinine
- Nicotine
- Chlorine
- Taurine
- Tartrazine
- Phenylalanine
- Cocaine
- Ibogaine
- Betaine
- DIM
- MDMA
- DMT
- LSD
- Ascorbic acid
- Most if not all prescription medication
- Carrageenan
- Aspartame

And here are some of the products that contain these horrific

substances:
- Carbonated beverages/sodas (caffeine, quinine, tartrazine, etc. Even the labels themselves will often warn the customer, saying: CAUTION: Contains caffeine)
- Energy drinks (caffeine, taurine)
- Shampoos (betaine. I use an egg as shampoo)
- Perfumes, deodorants and hand soaps (I use essential oils as deodorant, not baking soda, as some purists recommend. One drop of lavender is often enough)
- Protein powders
- Swimming pools (chlorine)
- Health powders and supplements (betaine)
- Chewing gum (phenylalanine, aspartame)

Beware also of acids and artificially produced vitamins. If you are unsure of whether or not the product is good for you, find out how the ingredients were processed. If solvents were used in manufacturing any of the individual ingredients, the product is karmic. Don't be tricked by the giants of industry.

Now let's take a look at the original ten commandments, the ones that were revealed by Jesus in the Essene Gospel of Peace. Though I have verified that these commandments are indeed the original ones, I have decided to decode them and put them here in plain language. I have of course used the guidance of Swedenborg and others, combined with my experience, to help me explain them:

1. Don't seek truth outside God

2. Don't let your personal will override the truth
3. Don't contradict the truth within
4. Love your body and your soul
5. Devote one day a week to solitude and silence
6. Don't kill a body or a soul
7. Don't spill your creative energy
8. Don't sell your soul
9. Don't tell lies
10. Don't want what doesn't belong to you

After many years, I came to the conclusion that the easiest way to avoid karma is to have a simple life because a simple life not only provides less opportunities for crime but also facilitates a more pleasant inner state. Complicated living usually leads to karma. "Be as simple as a dove and as prudent as a snake," said the Master.

Karma is easy to get because we are ignorant of so many things. Try not to break the law even in the littlest of ways. The biblical character James has a line about this, 2:10, saying, "Whoever keeps the whole law and yet offends in one point, is guilty of all." Simply your needs. Try not to do anything so unusual or outside the norm that it crosses the line, karmically. Try not to involve yourself in too many things.

Now I will leave you with the following story:

I went on a date with a girl who was compatible but, to my surprise, nothing came out of it. We found it difficult to approach each other. Months later, after losing her, she admitted to me that the obstacle was "a strange atmosphere between us." I believe it was this that stopped us from getting together. Now guess what that atmosphere was.

Creation

> *"To create the beloved, the beautiful,*
> *requires the highest art,*
> *the magic of luminaries."*
>
> — GOETHE, FAUST, PART TWO: ACT 1, 1832

Creation and attraction are synonymous, and that is why the best way to attract your soulmate is by having the laws of creation support you, which is done by complying with the following principles of Nature:

1. Ability to stand alone
2. Honesty of purpose
3. Devotion to God and to humanity

The first principle can perhaps be summarized in the following words of entrepreneur Rob Dyrdek: Just build a respectful clean life. To the dismay of everyone around him, Dyrdek stopped going out and starting living as though he were the perfect husband. Shortly thereafter, Dyrdek married his soulmate. Another way to understand this principle could be to ask yourself: If your parents were to leave you alone by yourself, how would you act? Would you misbehave or would you do the right thing? Standing alone requires you to know right from wrong but with respect to the laws of creation, there is yet another aspect to take into account: chastity. This and cleanliness are the aspects I elaborate in Part Two, because if you are unclean, and if you are spilling your creative energy, instead of standing you are falling.

The second principle is honesty, honesty in thought and continuity of purpose. Nature demands honesty above all things and grades us according to how honest we are with the knowledge we have. The more devoted we are to applying the truths that we know, the better. In Nature's eyes procrastinating would be dishonest because while we say we want one thing, our actions tell another story. To be really honest means to follow the right impulses we receive from within while putting our knowledge into action.

The third principle means to bring forth the light within oneself and to help people. Actually, if you do nothing else in this book, and if you don't want to work with all the principles simultaneously, then I have only one word for you: *give*. Giving is often all a person needs to find love. Now if giving isn't enough for you, then read on as I describe the rest of the process in greater detail:

First, you will need creative energy, which accumulates

naturally when one is chaste. Then you will need to tune your mind, heart and body to the force of love by moving in a straight line towards the goal, feeling conscious, getting clean, being generous and exercising regularly. Once these forces are in operation we will often come across a lustful member of the opposite sex who appears to desire us in an exclusively sexual way. By refusing to talk to this person, we are, shortly thereafter, granted an intuitive flash that if acted upon, lead to our soulmate. It's an uninterrupted series of sacrifices and efforts. Patience and perseverance are required elements throughout because in some cases the process takes longer than 40 days.

In 1924 Beinsa Douno revealed a formula that he said was worth 2 billion dollars. Failing to apply it would result in a $20 million fine. He was of course referring to karma and cosmic capital. The formula is as follows: "Warm heart, fresh soul, bright mind, strong spirit." A warm heart is a generous heart. Freshness of soul is felt by meditating or powering down the intellect. A bright mind is achieved by "going all in", through "total immersion, total obsession". A strong spirit creates and recreates things, and human creation is accomplished within us by standing firm in chastity. Notice that none of these four elements are about reading, learning or the consumption of art. Magic is about doing. But there is one thing to know once you begin creating your soulmate.

Prayer, or the communion of love, is somewhat automatic in one who meditates well as "prayer is a silence that penetrates the heart," but due to the promiscuous world we live in, I suggest you add a very specific request each day to protect your soulmate before you find them. If you do not make such a request, then what may happen is that your soulmate falls into the wrong relationship before you get to them. Here is how I suggest you formulate the request: "My Divine Father I beg you to protect my complements from every evil and wicked thought." Repeat 70 times each day, with feeling, and preferably with your barefeet on the ground while the sun is in the sky.

CLEANLINESS

THE FIRST CONDITION OF LOVE

"In one of the ancient esoteric societies of the past, when a member had attained to purity of thought and cleanliness of the person, he was symbolically married to one of the beings of the element of air."

— THE LORD GOD OF TRUTH WITHIN, ELEMENTAL HELPERS, 1941

Bodily cleanliness is one of the two conditions of the most demanding elemental marriages. The other is mental purity, which I address in the chapter on consciousness.

Cleanliness is common sense to those who say, "Who would marry someone filthy?" Though if these people were as clean as they imagined themselves to be, they would not fall ill in their fifties. Most people are loaded with parasites.

Cleanliness, real cleanliness, is actually quite rare and my intention in writing this chapter is to provide you with some secrets that are difficult to find elsewhere. I have noticed that by working with some of these secrets, something magical happens, it's as if the heart and everything within functions as it should, and this facilitates everything else.

Clean habits

1. Steam room twice a week. Steam rooms clean the pores. Be sure to drink salted water throughout the process.
2. Fast on garlic to clean the body of parasites, but only under professional supervision.
3. Do breathing exercises to clean your lungs. Inhale through the left nostril, then exhale through the right and inhale back through the right, and so on. Inhale/exhale to the count of 10 seconds. Morning, noon and night is ideal, but not more than five minutes at a time. The alternative is to inhale, hold, then exhale but only for a few seconds.
4. Mouthwash regularly. Try using wheat grass powder or coconut oil. Chewing Siberian or Mastic gum also helps.
5. At night, wash your hands and feet with hot water before going to bed.
6. Chew clean food well. Chicken is preferable to beef.
7. Wear clean clothes.
8. Drink clean water and try showering 2-3 times a day in clean water, or steam bathing instead.
9. A good massage can dislodge stubborn impurities.
10. Keep a vegetarian diet on the days you expect to find love. It is cleaner than eating meat.

CHASTITY

THE FOUNDATION OF LOVE

*"Nature is chaste, and it is to chastity
that she gives the keys of life."*

— ELIPHAS LEVI, THE KEY TO GREAT MYSTERIES, 1859

We are now about to reveal a secret that has remained somewhat hidden for thousands of years. One of the reasons it remained a secret for so long is because only a small number of people would take it seriously, people who yearn for superior things. Not everyone at school is interested in getting high grades and likewise not everyone is interested in superior levels of being. If you are not the spiritual type, you may want to skip this chapter and move onto the next – a suitable partner will probably appear regardless.

I now wish to address myself to those souls who yearn for something higher, something mysterious. Understand that it is inner love that attracts the soulmate but this love cannot really exist without some level of inner purity. Inner purity in itself does not make you attractive but it does lay the foundation for being attractive to others who yearn for the things you do.

Now what do I mean by purity? By purity I mean the opposite of lust, which is a virtue called chastity.

Chastity is not, as many people believe, a renunciation of sexual pleasures. Celibacy is one thing, chastity another. Excessive celibacy is dangerous, while excessive chastity is not. Chastity is a superpower that fights off lust. When this virtue is inwardly active it can feel like 'fresh air within'.

According to Apuleius, who veiled numerous love secrets in his books, the Eternal Mother revealed the necessity of chastity in her formula for transformation: "You will earn Our approval by intense discipline, spiritual service and firm chastity." The Eternal Mother, or Cupid, is the all-encompassing love-substance that has the power and the intelligence to direct a person's life in such a way that the soulmate arrives or departs.

Chastity is not about sexual repression, as repressing the raw sexual desire would only be harmful and counter-productive. We do not want to encourage the repression or expression of lust, but the observation of it.

By observing and increasing your awareness of these lustful thoughts and feelings, we shine a light onto these things, thereby understanding their hidden motive. A desire for sex does exist in pure lovers, it is just that they do not express it in a lustful, passionate and animal way, as so many others do. Pure lovers are different, they have sex, but they are loving one another, not selfishly using each other.

In the mind, chastity means to not indulge in sexual

thoughts – to not think them and to not stimulate them. In the heart, it means to not lust after a person or thing. In society, it means to not speak or act in a lustful way. In the body, it means to not have orgasms.

Orgasm has been misunderstood by humanity and we are now suffering the consequences. The majority of history's greatest teachers have outwardly revealed the harmful nature of orgasm but the amount of contemporary literature suggesting the opposite is so abundant that the classics have become obscured. Motivational messenger and author Preston Smiles had no orgasms for six months before he met his soulmate. Now let me quote from a handful of these teachers, but keep in mind that in the following quotes the word 'semen' does not refer only to the male sperm but to the sexual fluid in women too. Now let's get started.

The admired poet Kabir (1440-1518) said, "A dog, when it indulges in coition; it remains sad for a month, that affects it one month." The chastity of dogs is actually one of the secret reasons why they are often happier than humans. Galen (129-216 AD), the revered physician, added to this by saying, "All animals are sad after ejaculation, except women and roosters." I once showed this quote to a girlfriend of mine and it upset her because she did not feel it contained the whole truth, and she was right. For example, Marnia Robinson (b. 1954), respected author of Cupid's Poisoned Arrow, found that she would become moody about five days after orgasm, which suggests that the ejaculatory hangover does not happen at the same time for both sexes.

In 1988, the Dalai Lama, in his Survey on the Paths of

Tibetan Buddhism, said that ejaculation was a fault and that "further development" could not be made while ejaculating. Fortunately, he did reveal that sex was a necessary part of inner growth and some of his pupils are now teaching in the West with their somewhat secret wives.

Beethoven, one of history's greatest composers, who reportedly also had a secret wife, wrote: "Sensual gratification without a spiritual union is and will always be bestial, afterwards one has no trace of noble feeling but rather remorse." It is believed that Beethoven knew the secret to sex and the nature of orgasm. Even if that were untrue, who could ever believe that such beautiful music could have come from a chronic ejaculator?

Aristotle (384-322 BC), one of history's most well-known philosophers, said the following, "For the exhaustion consequent on the loss of even a very little of the semen is conspicuous because the body is deprived of the ultimate gain drawn from the nutriment...in most men and as a general rule the result of intercourse is exhaustion and weakness rather than relief, for the reason given."

Gurdjieff (1877-1949), renowned mystic and teacher, gave the exotic name of 'exioëhary' to sperm and called it a 'sacred substance'. The immortal Paracelsus called it the 'vital fluid'. Gurdjieff said that by removing the sperm from oneself one is existing 'inappropriately'. Gurdjieff himself was an enormously powerful and loving individual and those who have read his books will realize how superior in power he was to ordinary people. In 1938, during a meeting with some of his students, he said, "Happy are those who understand the function of the sperm for the transformation of their being. Unhappy are those who use it in a one-sided way." Along similar lines, Dr. Krumm-Heller (1876-1949), in his Thaumaturgy Course, said, "If a man can dominate his sexual instinct, energetically avoiding the orgasm, he will preserve all the magnetic forces accumulated in his body."

In the third book of the Torah, the Lord says to Moses, "If a man spills his semen, he should wash his whole body in water, and be unclean until the night."

According to the Book of Splendors, the mysterious ancient text that appeared in the late 1200s and that gave birth to Kabbalism, spilling the semen is regarded as ruinous.

Henry David Thoreau, the famous American essayist, wrote, "The generative energy, which, when we are loose, dissipates and makes us unclean, when we are continent, invigorates and inspires us. Chastity is the flowering of man; and what are called Genius, Heroism, Holiness, and the like, are but various fruits which succeed it."

Manu, who Hinduists and Theosophists believe to be the progenitor of the current human race, said in his book of laws, "…when a man has shed his semen he is cleaned by washing…"

Yogananda, the renowned mystic mentioned in the introduction, said, "Every drop of creative chemical fluid is said to contain the concentrated essence of eight drops of blood and the electric energy that would be contained in their thousands of blood corpuscles…To drive them out of the body foolishly (lured by the enemy sexual temptation) is to lose these soldiers of energy and mental power and to become a victim of the army of darkness, disease, weakness, fear, worry, dissatisfaction, melancholia, and even premature death."

In Leaves of Morya's Garden, a book telepathically communicated to Helena Roerich in 1925, we read: "If we compare two individuals, of whom one dissipates the vital substance while the other consciously conserves it, we will be amazed at how much more sensitive the spiritual apparatus of the second becomes. The quality of his labors becomes entirely different, and the quantity of his projects and ideas multiplies. The centers of the solar plexus and brain are being heated, as it were, by an invisible fire. That is why temperance is not a pathological renunciation but a sensible action."

In 1931 the anonymous mystic who wrote The Dayspring of Youth, said, "Our creative forces are made to be preserved and not dissipated; for stored energy is a wealth that can ennoble our characters."

Do not kill, do not steal, do not ejaculate, these are three of the main precepts that have remained consistent in all ancient teachings. These were precepts given to us by powerful beings who wanted to teach us how to live.

Lao Tzu, Goethe, Plato and many others were men who profited from a higher type of sexuality. We too could profit, if we gave it a chance.

But still I hear people of all ages and even teenagers say, "Plato, Jesus, the Dalai Lama, all these men are wrong. Listen to me."

Orgasm is a manifestation of lust, not of love, and not of

spirituality. Orgasm can give power to a negative person but it can only weaken those who are positive. Orgasm makes humans unlike angels.

Orgasm is pleasurable, but that doesn't make it right. Revenge is pleasurable. Even anger can be pleasurable. I find eating a box of donuts pleasurable. But I know how I'll feel tomorrow.

Much like exercise, it's not how you feel during but how you feel after that counts. Only conscious people can really feel the hangover after orgasm. A person who is 'psychologically asleep' is numb to it. That is why it is so difficult to prove esoteric truths to anyone, it really depends on their general level of awareness.

Teachers throughout history have tried to wake people up. Attempts have been made to help people see what is before them and feel what is within them. A Master once said that he tries to show people that when it rains, the streets are wet.

It has been taught that men should neither look at women lustfully nor touch them lustfully. I myself have been a victim of these 'disturbing radiations', so I know how a woman feels in such a situation, and it ain't nice.

Guys should know that looking at women all the time and curious glances are habits that need to be avoided. It takes effort over time and eventually becomes a new habit, a habit in place of the old one. Habits are replaced, not removed.

And guys, with regard to hugging or touching a woman, next time you do it, put an energy of giving into it, an attitude of love. Lust is a taking energy, and takes something from her, corrupts her, leaving her worse off. Love gives. Again, effort over time will install this new habit, this habit of 'giving when touching', and women will notice. Also, try not to say lustful things, make lustful comments. Flirtation is a common example of this. In love there are fun comments that are natural and sprout from the soul, they are not flirtation but a kind of warmth.

It should also be mentioned that we should not have a negative attitude towards lust. If we hate the enemy we support it. One leans on what resists.

Lust manifests in many ways. Observe. Be aware. Don't identify or give strength to the sexual thoughts that want your attention. Don't let lust have power over you. Again, lust should be observed, not repressed or expressed.

Self-observation is like a light that we shine onto our own darkness and by this light the darkness goes away.

With all these words I am not saying that lust needs to be overcome in its entirety in order for the soulmate to appear, because that would be impossible, but a certain portion of lust's superficial details should be overcome, at least to some extent.

Other lustful actions include masturbation, watching pornography and anything that stimulates the mind to lust.

Those who stop masturbating should know that in most cases when masturbation stops, wet dreams begin. Wet dreams are caused by a sexual thought that masturbation gave birth to. It has a life of its own and when self-indulgence has been absent for a while, the sexual thought gets hungry and starts to attack the mind during sleep, resulting in a wet dream. As long as the lust remains strong, it will always produce the urge to masturbate once more. As we have said, thoughts of any kind will lose their power over us if we observe them, and meditation helps this. That is why those who stop masturbating must seriously start the regular practice of meditation and self-awareness, so that the urge does not return. And then strategies must be utilized to prevent wet dreams. If the urge to "release" continues to plague your days, and if even your doctor is telling you to masturbate, the problem here is usually one of two things: your lustful thoughts are still very strong; or you are not utilizing the sexual energy in other ways.

The sexual energy is automatically utilized when we engage in sports and strenuous physical exercise (i.e. physical). It can also be redirected into creative work that we find interesting, such as drawing or writing (i.e. mental). The appreciation of beauty and music also utilizes the sexual energy (i.e. emotional).

People with lustful friends or those who frequent lustful environments, have a stronger chance of feeling the urge for orgasm. Of course, the remedy here is to avoid lustful places such as cinemas and nightclubs, and to clean one's body and home by burning things like sage and juniper berries.

People who are struggling with the masturbation habit may find help online at Reddit, a popular social news website. One of the communities hosted by Reddit is devoted to helping people overcome masturbation. The community is called No Fap. It has about 300,000 subscribers so you may find support and encouragement there.

Many people cannot tell the difference between love and lust. Some of us even have a lustful idea of love. If you look closely, you should be able to see who you truly love and who only appeals to your sexual desires. If you find it difficult to differentiate between love and lust, imagine this: imagine your idea of a man in love, who, by night, turns into a horny devil to devour his companion, with a lustful and sinister look on his face! Is this what you call love? I'm not sure how lust made its way onto a throne in this world but I do know that the misconception needs to be addressed.

It is said that forty drops of blood make one drop of semen. Forty days of no orgasms build a full reservoir of seminal energy, which is why it can often take time for cosmic souls to become truly attractive. Though in general, these things progress according to efforts and not time.

From my observations, time and magnetism play an important role in dating your soulmate but not so much in meeting each other for the first time. Let me give you an example of how this works in the case of a wet dream: a man meets his soulmate and they make a date for Thursday night. Unfortunately he has a wet dream the night before. Thursday comes and she cancels the date as she is suddenly not feeling well. Before he can see her again at least seven days have to pass from the last wet dream. So in this case no earlier than the following Wednesday. Wet dreams only repel love in a person of love. Fortunately this law does not apply to everyone.

In conclusion, the practical application of this chapter

revolves primarily around the avoidance of orgasms but particularly those created by wet dreams.

CONVICTION

THE MENTALITY OF LOVE

"Dattatreya had a strong will and so he created a woman by mere willing."

— SIVANANDA, SURE WAYS FOR SUCCESS IN LIFE, 1936

Have you ever been in such a heated state of wanting that you decide to throw all distractions to the devil and march straight to the goal? It's the highest state of conviction I know, and it is conviction that relates to the inner side of love.

In the process of creating the object of love, Nature is watching to see how honest you are with the process. How many times a day do you let the mind think about things that are not directly connected to the day's discipline? How many times a day do you indulge in activities that bear no relation to the goal at hand? Years ago I had read about honesty of mind and honesty of purpose, but I had not seen the connection between success and honesty until I threw all my energies at the goal. Up until then I was simply being dishonest. But when I went all in, within hours she called.

In 1939 Beinsa Douno said, "Make sure your thoughts do not contradict the laws of nature. Nature is very demanding. As soon as you enter into contradiction, she discards everything, she does not accept anyone. She has carried out thousands and millions of experiments and what she knows is perfect." The more I started reflecting on my own contradictions the more I started noticing dishonesty whenever I let my thinking contradict my goals. If my goal was to go on a low-Information diet, why was I even thinking about watching YouTube videos and reading books? These thoughts were short-circuiting my faith. I could feel it. I wasn't being honest. I lacked concentration, and it is concentration that stirs supply.

To rapidly achieve any goal, even that of the soulmate, interruptions need to be sacrificed. Every distraction, everything that does not belong to the work at hand, has to be renounced temporarily. Spiritual men call it absolute devotion and businessmen call it focus. First things must come first, and second things must cease to exist, at least until the goal is accomplished.

From an esoteric perspective, or that of the Master Paracelsus, faith is the most important element in accomplishing anything. He wrote, "If we accomplish anything whatsoever, it is faith that accomplishes it inside us and through us...but faith only acts effectively when it is strong and pure, not weakened by doubt, nor dispersed by secondary considerations. Whoever wants to utilize it must have only one aim in view." Sivananda likened such a faith to a divine will that man too could harness, saying, "If his will is pure and strong, man also gets the objects in the twinkling of an eye." To concentrate or to wander, that is the question—all or nothing. Businessman Ed Mylett, apparently worth $400 million, said that things started to change for him only when he decided to max out, to perform to his peak. The wise Eliphas Levi put it like this: "One only really wants a thing when one wants it with all one's heart, to the point of breaking ties with one's dearest affections for it; and with all one's energies, to the point of risking one's health, one's fortune, and one's life."

With regard to doubt, if you feel it creeping in, switch your posture to that of certainty by lifting your chest a little. You could also use the law of suggestion by telling yourself, I will, I can. You may even need to start forging the sense of certainty, of conviction, by behaving as though you have it. Forging a quality like certainty is like summoning its particles to the surface of our being, and in doing so consistently, we become in actual fact the quality we had been forging. It requires patience. Gurdjieff gave another tip, that of carrying a note with you and reading it throughout the day. The note could read, 'I have faith,' or you may want to read a quote about faith or love that really moves you. One of Beinsa Douno's reads as follows: "If you want to love, don't be afraid. If you want to be loved, don't doubt."

Therefore, organize what you know to be true into a simple weekly program, and then, by following through and obeying the program, these truths will begin to shine in your mind by the power of faith, for faith is a solar force that illuminates the mind when we put our knowledge and energy into action. It is a lesson apparently worth $500 million in dharmic capital, in cosmic currency, and that is perhaps why it works so well in attracting your soulmate.

Every morning make up your mind that you are going to be better. Step up, be enthusiastic yourself and move at the speed of light, for the wagon won't make it. Throw away any doubt, hesitation, confusion, uncertainty, and don't be a changeable person. Get really good at being faithful to the goal of love. Whenever I sense the seduction of distraction creep in, I bring my attention back to the task at hand. You may even want to use the law of suggestion by saying something like, "I am moving in a straight line." Again, don't let your thoughts drift away from your goal, nor your actions. In applying yourself completely, your intensity will reach such a point that its heat will attract your soulmate.

The planets do not stand still and neither should we. In constant rational motion is love and happiness. So if you want to have love, move like love. Commit to great action, for in great action is not only love but honesty, and honesty is an exercise of all hours and of all moments. It's about throwing doubts and interruptions away and going all in. It's as co-founder of Quest Nutrition Tom Bilyeu said, "You've got to do it with everything you got. Anything else is guaranteed failure." The sage Yukteswar promised the almighty power of creation to such a faith when he said, "Remember this: if you have within you that faith which is truly divine, and if there is something you desire that is not in the universe, it shall be created for you."

CONSCIOUSNESS

THE FEELING OF LOVE

"Your mind must be utterly still for yang and yin to come together."

— JOHN CHANG, THE MAGUS OF JAVA, 2000

Sexual attraction has always been misunderstood by the majority. Some say it is a beautiful body. Others say it is a joyful character. Esotericists say it is something else, something invisible. If sexual attraction were something visible, then we could see it and by seeing it we would know it. Therefore sexual attraction will always remain a mystery for most people because of the very fact that it can't be seen, it is of another world.

When I began studying magnetism and real sexual attraction, I experienced things that had no logical explanation. One day I was attractive and the following day I wasn't. I did not understand how that could be. My look and my dress had not changed but overnight my magnetism had.

A revelation on the topic came to me when reading one of Eliphas Levi's posthumous books. In it he said, "White magnetism is compassion and black magnetism is aversion." What he was saying was that in order to attract what is beneficial, we need to feel warm-hearted, compassionate. We attract inconvenient things by feeling aversive. For me this was ground-breaking. For a long time I believed that men were only attracted to a beautiful body and that women were attracted to a certain attitude and conversation. What I eventually discovered through my own experience was that sexual attraction is predominantly internal and that to be attractive one has to be feeling something inwardly. In other words, feelings attract. "Feel!" said the 18 year old Goethe, "and then choose a girl with a beautiful body and a beautiful soul who chooses you, and then you will be happy like me."

Now there are many people who love talking about how powerful our minds are and how thoughts create the world but in reality thoughts do not create the world and thoughts do not attract soulmates.

Let me share with you one of my many experiences on the subject of magnetism:

I sat at a coffee shop and kept to myself. It seemed like no one was interested in talking to me. No one had ever tried talking to me at a coffee shop and I did not think that my luck was about to change. I sat there and decided to force myself to feel compassion, as I wanted to see the effect. So I began really trying to feel warmth and love towards every person that passed by in the street, towards everything, even the inanimate objects nearby. After a few minutes of feeling this way, the girl next to me started talking to me with the intention of making a boyfriend out of me. As I was talking to her I forgot about my practice and my heart slowly returned to normal. The compassion gradually faded away. So by the end of the conversation she was no longer interested in me. Did you catch that? She was interested in me a minute ago, immensely, and now she wasn't. No, it wasn't something I said.

Ideally in order to attract your soulmate, you need to be feeling loving, conscious, open-hearted, warm, whatever you want to call it. The stronger the feeling of love, the more attractive you will be.

Jesus revealed a cosmic law when he said, "The more you have, the more will be given to you." The more love one has inside, the more love will be given to you, but if you do not have love within, even the love that you have attracted in the past will begin to move away from you. By loving a thing you will attract it. That is the law.

A friend of mine once made two turntables out of cardboard so that he had something to play with in his spare time. He loved music and would often play with his fake turntables, spinning the paper circles, while feeling a love for mixing and music. Before long, a friend of his arrived and gave him a couple of turntables for free. This is one of the cosmic laws of love applied to a material object.

In order for the heart to feel love all of the time and not just some of the time, a gradual increase in 'being' needs to take place.

All authors will tell you to love yourself. And it is sound

advice. No one can love you more than you love yourself. It is said that to love oneself is to yearn for inner growth, and this requires normality. Beinsa Douno's advice was simpler: "Don't do bad things, don't adopt bad habits, that is how to love yourself." I want to add to this by saying that if you do not take good care of yourself you won't have it within you to completely enjoy someone else. Instead you will feel as if something is lacking, and that something is of course within you.

Love, consciousness, the mind and happiness are all interconnected: love and happiness are qualities of the consciousness, and they surface to the degree that the mind is silent. That is why Francis Bacon said that love is the happiest state of mind. Now you will understand why various sages throughout history have said that meditation makes a person more magnetic, happier. The quieter the mind, the happier the heart. By not thinking we preserve mental energy, which can then be used in more productive ways.

It should be noted that thinking uses the same energy as doing, so the person who thinks a lot will naturally feel lazier than a person who doesn't.

Some people ask, "By encouraging not thinking are you encouraging ignorance?" Most people ask such questions because they do not understand the nature of knowledge. Knowledge comes from experience and intuition, not thinking. Do you know a lot about America because you have thought a lot about it? Thinking interferes with the clarity that leads to knowledge. The mind is the only real obstacle to love. The more we activate the mind, the less we feel. The interesting thing about all this is that the mind was not actually made to think, it was made to receive impressions. It was made to be receptive, not active. Its natural state is to be quiet, silent, like a deep and tranquil ocean. The thinking process is therefore an accident. Having said that, thinking, a certain type of thinking, can be useful when planning or studying, but it is not necessary to think in the shower, to think in the car, to think at the beach, to think all the time!

A word must be said about food because food has an enormous effect on the mind. All root vegetables make the mind think. Mushrooms make the mind reflect. Potatoes make the thoughts materialistic. Coffee and tea can also stimulate the mind. Pork needs to be avoided entirely as it can only add to a chaotic mind. Whenever you eat pork, you gain one thing and lose nine. Peanuts, due to the way they are stored, can often stir the mind. Fluoridated water makes the mind less perceptive. Meat with added hormones, cooked honey, all these things can get in the way of a clear mind, but our choice of lifestyle is also important.

Leave behind the intellectual lifestyle and adopt a feel-good lifestyle. Live simply. Don't think much. Avoid immersing yourself in the world of books and computer screens. Meditate, engage in a vibrant social life, be more aware, spend more time in nature, eat healthy, avoid intellectual activities, all these things can make you feel more conscious. Free yourself from the intellect and the feeling of love will begin to surface in a natural way. Love yourself, look after yourself, and don't do what you hate.

I have only been able to achieve love-magnetism reliably by a steady routine of daily meditation. Yogananda said, "Through meditation, unmarried people can learn to sublimate the emotions and unite the creative nature force with the soul force, thus creating within themselves a mighty magnetism, which will draw to them their soul's companion if they wish to marry." Through meditation we contact God by experiencing peace, and by contacting God your soulmate will contact you, for sex is the doorway to heaven.

Francis Bacon described the state that attracts love as follows: "When our minds are soundest, when they are not, as it were, in sickness and therefore out of taste, but when we are in prosperity, when we want nothing, then is the season, the opportunity, and the spring of love." In short, the ones who sacrifice their intellect are the ones who experience love. The implications are that you don't have to meditate to experience the inner state of love, but you do have to set yourself free from your intellect by, for example, eliminating books, discarding information, or controlling your intellectual curiosity.

When the mind stops searching, when it no longer wants shelter, when it no longer goes in search of safety, when it no longer craves more books and information, when it now ignores even the memory of desire, only then does that which is called Love arrive within us, for as the poet Ovid wrote, *Venus otia amat,* Venus loves peace.

Resources for meditation:
- Headspace: an app to help you meditate
- Noise canceling headphones to reduce ambient noise
- Get a comfortable sleep mask
- Get a comfortable La-Z-Boy recliner
- Paint the walls of your meditation room with EMR shielding paint

CHARITY

THE ACT OF LOVE

"Sage and I are a natural match. We have the same values and beliefs... She's my karma for being able to help people."

— TONY ROBBINS, INTERVIEW WITH GLENN PLASKIN, 2013

To love is to give, which is why giving attracts love. Giving, or charity, is actually a law of nature with a thousandfold return. It is an obligation of man neglected by most. But not all giving is equal in value.

To help your friends is to help yourself. It is the law of mutual assistance. Even criminals apply this law by helping their friends and family. But towering above mutual assistance is an even greater law called universal assistance, which means helping strangers, or people who cannot give back. Because if you only give to your friends and family, how are you any different to the criminals who do the same?

Swedenborg said many things about charity but the line

that struck me the most was: "Good deeds hold charity, which holds love for the Lord, which holds the Lord himself." In other words, charity possesses divine wisdom and the charitable person should not be surprised to find their soulmate in the days to come, for divinity is now rearranging things according to the dictates of wisdom.

Helping people also makes us happier, so the rational argument would be that if you want to attract a happy sexual relationship you would have to do things that not only make you sexier but happier.

Karmic laws play a critical role in the soulmate process, and that is why past mistakes can slow the process down. If all you've been doing for the past decade is pill-popping and bed-hopping, then charity can help in canceling some of that karma for you.

I know a woman who slept with so many of the wrong men that she feels burdened by her karma. She feels as if karma will not let her have a loving relationship. This may be true right now but it is false to assume that it is incurable. Almost all karma can be erased by right thinking, right feeling and right doing. Help a friend. Help your family. Give with love. Give without any expectation of reward. But please, when giving to the homeless, give food, not money. "If ye would have love, love others," said Edgar Cayce. But know that we also help by our mental and emotional states.

A wise man once that thoughts and feelings travel the world and that if for example we were today to feel particularly compassionate we could be unknowingly stopping acts of violence on the other side of the planet. I still remember how everything around me seemed to change for the better after I decided to focus on feeling good by meditating and denying intellectual stimuli. Annie Besant addressed this phenomenon when she said, "A man is what he desires and thinks, and not what he does. What he desires and thinks shapes his future; what he does is the outcome of his past. Actions are the least important part of a man's life, from the esoteric standpoint — a hard doctrine to many, but true." In the context of charity, what Annie is saying is that actions are important but thoughts and feelings even more so. Does that mean that we should allocate more time for ourselves than we do for others? That is the question and the answer may vary depending on your personal situation. In any case, charity gives us an advantage. It makes the soulmate appear faster. And though it may seem that a feeling of love is more powerful than an act of love, both are necessary.

Now I want to share with you a few of my own stories about the magnetic power of charity:

- One night I gave my only spare quilt to a homeless person and an hour later a beautiful woman contacted me wanting to meet up.
- Once I spent the whole day doing things for family and friends and before the day was over, I experienced 'love at first sight.'
- Once I wanted to show a friend of mine an educational video on the Internet and at one of the computers nearby I met a girl with whom there was an instant and beautiful attraction.
- After four consecutive days of giving food to the less

fortunate I came across a girl who took me dancing that very night and who exhibited all the signs of a soulmate.

As you can see, charity has a secret power. Just don't let it take over your life and do not go to such extremes that you yourself are left without. Now if you're wondering how to apply this principle, here are my nine best suggestions:

1. Give food to the homeless (physical)
2. Cheer up the lonely people at the nursing home (mental)
3. Teach deserving people new ideas (mental)
4. Host workshops in which you have attendees dissolve their egos (spiritual)
5. Apply the Padma Purana formula (vedic)
6. Each Friday, fast (dharmic)
7. Each Saturday, practice absolute verbal silence (dharmic)
8. Any lack of mercy frustrates the soulmate process. Whenever asked, give. I am not suggesting you give money but food. In practice this implies that you prepare by carrying food items with you in case you get asked. Gurdjieff carried bonbons, Sivananda suggested pies, and Beinsa Douno muffins. If a beggar petitions you and you give nothing, you short-circuit the soulmate process.

To quote a Buddhist precept, "Never put food into the mouth of the hungry by the hand of another." In the past I would donate organic milk and juice but the rewards were slow and the destitute didn't always appreciate the healthy food. Most of them don't even know what healthy food is, not do they care to know. Nowadays when I give food I buy things like sandwiches and pies that are more or less healthy.

It's not something that I myself would eat but it's nourishing and they enjoy it. Is it toxic? A little, but it's better than staying hungry. My suggestion is to design a circuit that you can travel each day and predictably find people to feed. Unless you have plenty of money to splash around, limit what you spend on food to six percent, which was Sivananda's recommendation. He said, "Do charity regularly, every month, or even daily according to your means. Never fail in this item. If necessary forgo some personal wants but keep up this charity regularly."

If you don't have a lot of money for food or if beggars are scarce in your area I suggest you find a nursing home that you can attend regularly, giving 90-120 minutes of your companionship but only to the lonely people who seem to benefit from it. The reason why I suggest limiting your time is because you don't want to exhaust the person. Ask him or her about their way of being, their family and try sharing something beautiful with them to cheer them up. I credit this approach to the Buddhist Michael Roach. A student of his met her soulmate within months of using this approach.

If dissolving the darkness is a technique you're familiar with, why not guide others through the process? Of all the forms of charity that I've practiced none bring luck so thick and fast as this one. And if you're still not convinced that luck can be caused by charity, let me take you back to the 13th century and quote for you the Viking saga of Gautrek: "Good luck to a generous man!" Though be sure not to tell anyone about your charitable deeds, or else you will be reducing your reward by half.

If instead of my suggestions you would rather apply the formula of the Hindu text Padma Purana, here it is:
1. Each day chant a mantra
2. Each day feed at least one starving beggar
3. Each day give a small amount of food to animals
4. Each week give knowledge to deserving people
5. Each week help your parents or the elderly

Now, with regard to fasting and its relation to charitable rewards, I want to start by quoting Jesus: "Go by yourself and fast alone, and show your fasting to no man. The living God will see it and great shall be your reward."

In fasting lies fortune, for some. After two 40-day fasts, Ghandi liberated India, and Beinsa Douno claimed that Ireland was liberated in the same way. I even know of a woman who saved her husband's life, and miraculously so, after a 40-day fast. Jesus even alluded to the fact that each day of subsequent fasting and meditation could erase one year of karmic debt, and karma, being the law on which all things depend, is the key to the soulmate process. Actually, in 1966 Samael Aun Weor went so far as to suggest that it was karma that was secretly responsible for our failures in finding love, writing, "Only the total and perfect complement can grant us inexhaustible happiness; unfortunately it's a lot to ask, we don't deserve so much, we are all full of karma." Thankfully karma can be counteracted and one of the easiest ways to do so is to fast.

The first time I discovered the connection between karma and fasting, was when I was scrambling for money in one of the darkest periods of my life. Months earlier I had met my soulmate but even with all the charity I was doing, I had not managed to see her even once. Other girls had also been appearing and in my ignorance I was denying all of them. I had no money and oftentimes I would go for walks in nature and feel an impending sense of doom. I was clearly in a terrible situation and I had no solution in sight, all because of a curse. A curse had been imposing itself on my life and though I had come to accept it as normal, it seemed to have reached a point of crippling me, so I got desperate. I asked a wise man for help and though he did not respond physically, I may have received a response telepathically because shortly after, I found what I was looking for in one of the most interesting lines I had ever read in over ten years of research: "If you eat on a Friday, you will get into trouble, it will cost you thousands of years." This quote struck me like lightning and so I decided to try it, as I had nothing to lose.

On my first Friday fast, I drank only hot water. Towards the end of the day I decided to leave home to visit the city, and noticed something very strange. My neighborhood seemed quieter. When I arrived in the city, I noticed that the city itself also felt quieter, but what I was actually sensing was a newfound peace within me. I was finally at peace with God, or so it seemed. That night, in my dreams, a stranger's girlfriend kissed me, which had never happened to me before. I then began to notice girls paying more attention to me during the day and even the girlfriends of others. Beinsa Douno once said that as soon as a man pays his debts, he should anticipate a wife. My fast had paid the interest on my debts for that week, and that was all I needed to make a breakthrough.

In Homer's Odyssey, we see the gods rewarding only the men who sacrifice something of value. Debts have to be paid and self-sacrifice is the way to do it if you cannot pay them now in full. If you owe money, or sense a need to fast, here are some guidelines:

- Stop eating on Thursday 6pm latest and start again on Friday, 27 hours after the last mouthful. This matters.
- Drink spring water, preferably heated by the sun and from glass bottles. Add high-quality salt to the water.
- Do not go for long walks during a fast.
- Do not tell anyone that you are fasting.
- Refrain from negative thoughts or feelings during a fast. Refrain from indulging in all the bitterness of the Earth. Instead, consider singing and thanking Nature for what you have.
- Only use clean words during a fast.
- During a fast, meditate.
- Go to a steam room before fasting, to unblock the pores.
- Do not fast if you are too scared to do so.
- Do not fast if you have better ways to pay your debts.
- Diffuse essential oils during a fast so that you are fed through the air.
- Fast only if you can afford to lose a little weight. If you need to gain weight before fasting, the healthy way to do so is to eat fruit every hour between your four meals a day.

In 1920 Beinsa Douno said that since the time of Christ

we have had to fast one day a month to give our stomach a rest. Now if we calculate the number of days we owe the stomach since the Christic drama took place, it would be 24,000, which is about 65 years. This is a karmic load that could be nullified by fasting 5 days a month, which is worth about $800,000 in cosmic capital. The karmic debt could also be paid by using a lot of your own money to help a lot of people, or perhaps even by dissolving a lot of egos or having others do the same. Beinsa Douno declared that one of the main secrets as to why people suffer is because of this enormous debt that is not being paid off. He said that if you are going to eat on Fridays, eat round fruits that are pink or red, like cherries, apples, tomatoes, or strawberries. But the whole point of this is to please Homer's gods by sacrificing food on Fridays. Alongside the steam room I believe this is one of the greatest practices revealed in this book.

As you probably already know, the influence of Venus is strongest on Fridays, making it the day of love. But what most people don't know is that all the evil in the world comes from the sexual decadence, aka the crimes of love, of our remote ancestors. Jesus knew about this, which is why he chose to sacrifice his body on a Friday and not on other days. The easiest way to relieve ourselves temporarily from this ancestral karma may be to finish a 24 hour fast on a Friday, which would begin on a Thursday, e.g. from Thursday noon to Friday noon. The longer the fast, the more debt is paid off.

Refraining from speech is another way to pay off karmic debt and the best day to do this, astrologically speaking, is on a Saturday. I personally find it very difficult to not let my mouth make any sound for a whole day, but I like the challenge.

Whichever way you decide to give, make sure it happens, but think it through first.

Lastly, consider these words from the first book of Leaves of Morya's Garden: "Do not eat from the table of the Lord, but hearken to His Words." With charity you will be earning dharma and with consumption you will be spending it. If you are giving a lot while taking a lot, you are not allowing love to enter your life, for your consumption of the good is too great. I have a saying for this: No good is received unpunished. Even all the free things consumed or done for you is subtracted from the cosmic capital you have accumulated. Keep this in mind moving forward. Receiving too much holds back the reception of love. Free services like YouTube and Facebook consume dharma. Free services cost real money.

BEAUTY

THE CONQUERER OF LOVE

"I have religiously continued my daily workout for 14 years now, and know they contribute immensely to the magnetism that attracted my dream woman, Deypika, to me."

— VISH IYER, YOGA AND LOVE, 2013

Everybody intuitively knows how much sway a beautiful body has over another. It is like an external symbol of love, in that through your body you show the world how much you love yourself. Similarly, someone who drives a car that is dirty and beaten up exhibits something of himself to the world.

Sivananda implored his students to develop a beautiful symmetrical body, but why? Because no culture, not even that of perfect love, is possible without a physical culture. While long hours of meditation can awaken the beauty within, exercise combined with a correct diet can lead to the beauty without. "An unshapely form exhibits neglect," says one. "If you cannot love your body then how will you love mine?" says another.

The body is made beautiful by exercise, the face by food and love. The beauty of the mouth is formed by the love of love; that of the nose by the love of wisdom, and that of the eyes by the love of truth.

Years ago while in New York I decided to try a pasteurized juice made of apricot puree, peach puree and apple juice. I drank about one liter. The very next day I woke up with a complexion and a radiance that drew the attention of complete strangers. Even beautiful women approached me. I had stumbled across my first beauty-food.

In A Midsummer Night's Dream, Shakespeare mentions five foods in relation to "purging one's mortal grossness":

1. Apricots
2. Berries
3. Purple grapes
4. Green figs
5. Honey

Beinsa Douno also noted some beauty-foods:

1. Prunes
2. Apples
3. Peas

Sivananda revealed only one beauty-food that I know of:

1. Solanum Trilobatum

These foods may require one lunar cycle, or 30 days to take effect. And some will require a whole year. After carrying out my own experiments, here are the beauty-

foods I've enjoyed the most:
1. Apricot juice
2. Nettles
3. Blueberries or crowberries
4. Prunes
5. Egg yolks

Once I started exercising I noticed that my soulmate would hang around a little longer. There was a type of bond established that wasn't there before. In the past the absence of exercise seemed to correlate with the absence of this binding agent, this glue in our relationship, and so these relationships always dissolved. Before starting a workout routine there was nothing to cement the desire. Meditation wasn't enough, and after reading the words of Jesus, I knew that I had to start loving my body.

With regard to grooming, adjust your hairstyle, physical appearance and clothing to match the ideal that your soulmate would be looking for. I am not suggesting you dress like someone else. Some people do not dress or look the way they want because they mistakenly regard fashion or grooming as inferior things. Perhaps pay a little more attention. Wear clothes that fit.

If you believe that your soulmate is the type of person to desire a beautiful body, exercise regularly. Don't let an unshapely form frighten the opposite sex. Don't risk repulsing your purest dreams.

Being healthy implies that you can also look after the health of another person. It is not necessary to be perfectly healthy to meet your soulmate but being healthy aids in beauty and action. Knowing what I know about health has helped me so much in life that I feel obliged to share my keys with you here, because organic food will only get you so far. Eighteen years of personal research has culminated in only fourteen principles, some of which are dangerous to the inexperienced:

1. Steam rooms unblock the pores while removing stress and radiation
2. Essential oils if diffused will enter those pores, thereby infiltrating the bloodstream with Nature's intelligence
3. Placing your palms and barefeet on the earth from 8-9am nude in the sunlight draws in the intelligence of the Earth and the Sun. And getting rained on increases your magnetism
4. Garlic fasts remove parasites and restore youthfulness
5. Eat clean, and consider adding cracked cell wall Chlorella, St John's Wort powder, salted water, magnesium-rich seeds, zinc-rich pine pollen, and organic beef liver
6. Rhythmic breathing, aiming eventually at 10-30-10.
7. In answering nature's call, squat don't sit
8. Wear a newly earthed copper bracelet for cell phone protection
9. Classical music. Life begins with music and ends with the termination of music
10. Ultramassage
11. Lampe Berger neutral destroys airborne bacteria and house odors
12. Sing even in moments of distress
13. Chew Siberian gum after meals

SUGGESTION

THE SUBCONSCIOUS LAW OF SUCCESS

*"When you learn the Law of
Suggestion and apply it in every area
of your life, then you will succeed in
everything."*

— BEINSA DOUNO, AUGUST 29, 1926

Now it is time to get moving a little faster towards success. For this we will need our body, heart and mind, and there are laws for each of these.

- Mind: The Law of Suggestion (S)
- Heart: The Law of Intuition (I)
- Body: The Law of Action (A)

The Law of Suggestion is associated with the past, the Law of Intuition with the future, and the Law of Action with the eternal now. When all three laws are applied, success is guaranteed, for success is the outcome of right (I) actions (A) and thoughts (S). This three-sided approach was something I had intentionally ignored, and consequently, doom and gloom found its way to my doorstep. Up until that point I thought that as long as I took action and obeyed my intuition I would succeed. I was wrong. What I discovered was that there was a secret part of me, submerged within me, that had been working against my success without my consent. Wise men were calling it the subconsciousness, and Gurdjieff went so far as to say that the science of influencing the subconsciousness is the only science that we are absolutely needing, and which alone may perhaps even save us from abnormal impulses like procrastination. Actually, Napoleon Hill agreed, saying that self-suggestion holds the key. In my case it was not only my own words but those of others.

The first time I remember having my subconsciousness altered was while using the Internet. I was sitting down at my computer paying little attention to the webinar I had playing in the background. It was the enthusiastic voice of a married woman. A single friend of mine had sent me the link. As I was gazing at the screen not wholly aware of what the woman was talking about, one of her phrases jumped out at me, saying, "...you will fail in everything you do." The instant she said this, I felt my whole body vibrate in resonance with the command. It wasn't even intentional. It happened suddenly and without my participation. My subconsciousness had received the command and was now determined to make me fail, in everything.

Only a few weeks later, I met my soulmate and wrote down her number on a piece of paper. By the time I got home I had lost the paper. I then booked a videographer and he canceled on me twice. I decided to book another but this time I was the one who had to cancel as I busted my toe days before the shooting. At this point I started to suspect that my subconsciousness had orchestrated the entire series of tragedies. A secret part of me was keeping me from my success. That's when I started using the law of suggestion consciously, and, as it turns out, I was very late to the game, as many others had already used it with great success decades ago.

Mycologist Paul Stamets had been stuttering his whole life until he began repeating "Stop stuttering now" during a lightning storm. Billionaire Tony Robbins had little money until he began repeating phrases like "God's wealth is circulating in my life." One of Yoganada's students had been experiencing recurring financial disaster until he began repeating "Day by day I am getting better and better." When Beinsa Douno was once asked how something is accomplished, his whole response was, Give it to your subconscious mind and forget about it. Even Zig Ziglar, one of the great American salesmen, attributes his success largely to repeating subconscious commands twice a day.

Gurdjieff, Yogananda, Sivananda, Beinsa Douno, Esko Jalkanen, all awake, gave us various clues as to how to reprogram our minds for success, and for me they worked! After using them I got back in touch with the girl whose number I had lost and even ended up working with the videographer. It all happened after I started repeating the following rhyme:

> Perfume of success-thought
> blows in me, blows in me.
> I am charming and magnetic.
> I can do everything, I am free.

This rhyme is my shortened version of Yogananda's subconscious program for psychological success. It was composed for those who've been suffering from constant failure. Alternatively, if you are older, you may prefer:

> Perfume of success-thought
> blows in me, blows in me.
> I can do all that God can do.
> I will rejuvenate, I am free.

If you believe that you have been negatively programmed, as most people seem to be, then choose one of the rhymes above, or craft your own using existing phrases given by true sages. Much like popular songs, rhymes stick in the mind easier, that is why Yogananda advised us to use whole rhymes instead of stand-alone phrases. Start by saying it loudly a few times, then more softly, then whispering, then mentally, then subconsciously, and finally superconsciously.

The best way to use these rhymes to reprogram your subconscious mind is to repeat them while gazing at a shiny object. Gurdjieff said that any other way would be dangerous. Here is how I did it: I shined a very bright lamp onto my copper bracelet, and gazed at it until I began feeling drowsy, which for me would take about five minutes. Gold could be used, silver, turquoise or something else. You may prefer to have suggestions repeated while you use your computer, as a computer screen is also a shiny object, right?

Another way to reprogram your mind, though often less accessible, would be to shake hands with happy people who already have their soulmates. The effect would only last for three days, but hopefully three days is all you will need. Hand shakes bring their thoughts into you.

Interestingly, by studying people and their 'reference groups' over a 30 year period, Dr David McClelland of Harvard University discovered that 95% of our success or failure is determined by the people we habitually associate with. In high-level sport, most coaches and athletes will readily admit that 50 to 95 percent of success is due to mental factors. Therefore if you cannot access the people with the mentality that you'd like to acquire, self-hypnosis is perhaps your best alternative.

Start by repeating the rhymes while gazing at a shiny object, before noon or before falling asleep. You can also repeat individual phrases whenever you are feeling particularly inspired, in the best mood, in the highest spirits. Actually, for a lot of people the emotional part is so important that even Yogananda wanted us to take note of it when he said, "Words saturated with sincerity, conviction, faith, and intuition are like highly explosive vibration bombs, which, when set off, shatter the rocks of difficulties and create the change desired." But know that in life whatever you do, you can't get rid of the law of suggestion—it is far too powerful.

No mortal, even immortal, is free from it. Both the angels and the gods are under its positive influence.

Now if you want to incorporate this law into other aspects of your life, here are some ideas: Before any task, before any doubt, you could say, "I can do this, I can think rightly, I can be good." Whenever looking at yourself in the mirror, you could say, "As I am created, I am pleased, though there are things I have to develop. In any case I will work and make efforts to acquire something new." Instead of complaining about your conditions, you could say, "For my current development, I cannot expect better conditions than the ones I have. By working with love and joy I will be given better ones." All the while keep in mind that the subconsciousness has a life of its own. Don't upset it by trying to force it. Once you have it operating alongside you to accomplish your goals, back off and let it drive you from within.

If you want to learn more about the Law of Suggestion, here are some resources:
- Watch a professional hypnotist change a man's subconsciousness in a matter of minutes: https://youtu.be/2dJ3-N0HL4A (2015)
- Christie Marie Sheldon's technique to obliterate bad hypnosis: https://youtu.be/AENkBl0tp5E
- Scientific Healing Affirmations (1924) by Yogananda
- Beyond Willpower (2015) by Dr. Alexander Loyd is a contemporary manual loaded with techniques to change the subconsciousness.

- The Big Leap by Dr. Gay Hendricks
- Hypnotism (1950), chapter 32 in Gurdjieff's book, Belzebuub's Tales.
- The Power of the Subconsciousness and the Superconsciousness (January 17, 1934) by Beinsa Douno. This lecture is only available in Bulgarian. In it he gives many clues but what he alludes to is that unless your goals are in your subconsciousness and superconsciousness, they cannot be accomplished.

INTUITION

THE SUPERCONSCIOUS LAW OF SUCCESS

"Only when there has fallen the stillness of a silence that can be felt, only when the very air is motionless and the calm is profound, only when the man wraps his face in a mantle which closes his ears even to the silence that is of earth, then only sounds the voice that is stiller than the silence, the voice of his true Self."

— ANNIE BESANT, THE SEVEN PRINCIPLES OF MAN, 1892

There is a power so brilliant, so necessary, that even the greatest entrepreneurs have been showing it praise. Its role is interpenetration. Its purpose is guidance. Its name is intuition.

Intuition is the seventh sense. Imagination is the sixth. Imagination is inner seeing, intuition inner knowing. Intuition is felt in the heart as a hunch and can appear in the mind as an idea or an image. Intuition is always right because it is the voice of the Source that knows all things.

Intuition is transmitted to us by a extraordinary atom located at the root of the nose, the front of the brain, which is why people who have undergone frontal lobotomies are, among other things, unable to make decisions, because they no longer have the intuition they were utilizing to make these decisions.

If you are attractive enough, you will often find your soulmate due to the magnetism that has the power of creating opportunities and rearranging people. But if your circumstances prevent you from leading a normal social life, make a conscious effort to do one of these three things:

1. Follow your intuition
2. Follow your real interests by going places you love (or by staying home if that's what you genuinely prefer)
3. Accept invitations

Fanatics tend to believe that the soulmate will appear when the time is right, that God will take care of it and that no deliberate effort needs to be made to enter society. This may be true in some cases but there are some people who live such introverted lives that no Cupid can enter. By following your hunches you will always be in the right place at the right time; by visiting places you love, you are more likely to come cross your soulmate, as your soulmate loves the same places you do; and by accepting invitations, you can, much to your surprise, find yourself where your soulmate is.

You can also find your soulmate before attending an appointment or while on your way somewhere. Actually, many people follow their intuition accidentally. We naturally and unconsciously utilize our intuition everyday. Have you ever woken up in the morning and had an idea of how you want to spend the day? This idea may be intuitive and it may lead to finding your soulmate. So as the day progresses pay attention to any ideas that flash in the mind.

On one occasion, while driving down the street in a mentally calm state, an image suddenly flashed in my mind accompanied by a sensation that the message in the image was correct. The image was of a familiar dance school. I went there that night and met a girl with whom there was an immensely profound attraction, the most profound I had experienced in 30 years. At the time I was ignorant of the other principles in this book so nothing came of it.

The magnetism of consciousness brings your soulmate to you. The faculty of intuition brings you to them. Here is how to develop this faculty:

Vocalize, either internally or externally, the sound 'O' (as in 'door') for 20-60 minutes each day, while visualizing a small golden disc spinning over your heart, which would spin anti-clockwise if someone were looking at you. Analyze the illustration in Leadbeater's book The Chakras to know exactly what the intuition chakra looks like and where it is.

In the serenity of thought, intuition is noticed. When the doors to fantasy are closed, the organ of intuition awakens. Try to get out of your head and feel those hunches that are often ignored. I don't think, therefore I intuit. Try to push your mind into a space of non-thinking and feel to which place you should go.

So there you go! Stay aware and pay attention to any nudges you may get from within. Honor your curiosities and go places you love. And if you receive an invitation from a friend, accept it! Cultivate a childlike wonder while feeling and following your real interests. The two of you may pass each other on the street. You may spot each other on the bus, the subway, in a library, a city square, a grocery store, maybe even at a dance class.

Sometimes one must travel

> *"There are yet other lands*
> *where love will be truer."*

— *Zanoni, from Edward Bulwer-Lytton's book, 1842*

If you have undergone the process outlined so far and have not succeeded, I can only suggest two things: either give more or travel. Grant Cardone only met his soulmate after moving to a different city. Therefore, either revisit the chapter on charity or consider traveling to another city or even another country, preferably where you can continue applying the process. In other words, if you feel as though all your opportunities have evaporated in your home country, go elsewhere but not without seeking guidance first. Ask the Divine Wisdom within you. Here is one way you could formulate the request: "Oh Father, Mother, Friend, Beloved God, guide my reason, will, and activity to the right thing

I should do in everything." Make this emotional demand every day until you get a response. For me the guidance comes in dreams. And sometimes I can feel intuitively whether or not I belong in a certain place. But above all I find that guidance comes before I even ask and it comes only if I am sufficiently pure. A diamond requires a certain level of clarity in order for the light to penetrate.

Beinsa gave us a clue as to which location might be our ideal when he said, 'Live where the people love you twice as much as you love them.' He went on to say, "The law of opulence states that the conditions or the best elements or the best means for your life are invested somewhere in Bulgaria or France or Germany, or finally somewhere in America and you have to go right at this point in time to take them up, but you should not go earlier because you will have to wait, nor should you be late."

In addition, consider the following piece of advice from the philosopher Marsilio Ficino, who published this in 1489: "It is worth finding out exactly what place your star and your guide initially chose for you to live in and grow, because they will favor you more there. Assuredly, it is that place where, once you arrive, your soul is in some way thoroughly refreshed, where your sense stays strong, where your health is more vital, where the majority favor you more, where your wishes come true."

Look for guidance in your dreams. If you find nothing, ask your Creator to give you guidance through a dream, demand it. Keep asking with deep feeling, without ever getting tired of asking. And if you can't pray for yourself, ask someone to pray for you. The dreams that will bring the response are often the result of three things: intense inner work, going to bed early, praying consistently. It can even happen that a person astral projects into their home and discovers written guidance on the entrance door.

If all else fails, develop your intuition and then use it to feel through your options.

ACTION

THE SELFCONSCIÓUS LAW OF SUCCESS

"The man must approach first, with honesty in his words, and she will receive his flattering prayers kindly."

— OVID, THE ART OF LOVE, BOOK ONE, 2 AD

In order for two people to meet, they must talk. And I know this may sound hard to believe but there are some people who believe that when the time is right, the soulmate will fall out of the sky and into their lives with little or no effort whatsoever. Some men tell themselves, 'I do not need to talk to her because God will make it that she talks to me.' This is not always true. Personal initiative, or action, is almost always necessary.

There are some men who do not make enough efforts to meet the women who want to meet them. Others give up too easily. The multimillionaire and influential Grant Cardone called his wife once a fortnight for over a year before she agreed to meet with him. For bestselling author

Bob Goff it was over 3 years. They understood the value of being proactive and also the power of perseverance. God cannot do for us what we must do for ourselves.

You may have a mutual friend to introduce the two of you. You may be part of a social group in which communication occurs effortlessly. You may not have to initiate contact yourself. Regardless, you will have to talk to each other at some point so if you are particularly shy, work on it.

In some cases, when meeting someone new, you need to have a way of finding out whether or not the two of you are similar, before committing to contact them. Confirm common interests before deciding to take it further. It may be a casual question you ask them on the spot, it may be a story that you like to tell in order to get them to reveal their thoughts on the subject. Otherwise it can happen that you are so overloaded with phone numbers that concentration on any one of them is impossible. If you have no way of knowing outside dating them, it may work against you. Consider the following example: Mike meets Catherine, his soulmate, but he doesn't know yet. A few days pass and he meets other women and then one of these women begins desiring him. He then goes to call Catherine and she won't answer her phone nor will she respond to his texts. This is happening because one of the other women is blocking out Catherine by desiring Mike. A simple solution to this problem for men is to meet one woman at a time and to date this one before moving onto another. This means that no female friends can be made in the meantime. Some people may find this solution convenient but if time is pressing then you need to know now and not in a few weeks.

Oftentimes the woman provokes the man by the use of a gesture, the man then understands this gesture and approaches her. It takes two to tango. The woman will not do all the work. The woman provokes the man to approach, and when she provokes it is often instinctive.

For women, the practice of this chapter involves provoking the man to act by using a stare, a smile, a laugh, a whisper, etc. For men it's to talk.

Before concluding this chapter, I do have one unusual piece of advice for the men who are lacking in magnetism: if you have a moment before approaching the woman, recite the following formula three times, it will bring positive forces to your side and influence even a stubborn woman to be more receptive to your words:

We have the right in this world to grow and mature
This is a divine process, determined by God
No one has the right to stop this divine process within us
No power in the world has the right to retard our
development
It is in the Divine Plan that I develop
Therefore, I am on the path of Truth and Divine Life
This right no one can take from me. It is my own right
Where the Lord is, there I am also.

It is also interesting to know that soulmates will rarely meet for the first time on a negative astrological day. The intelligent force that brings soulmates together is not going to do so when the planets are sending forth negative radiations. Instead of going out every day with the hope of finding your soulmate, I suggest you use a vedic calendar to know in advance which days are astrologically positive, and if you eat meat like I do, be vegetarian on those days at least until you find your soulmate and exchange numbers, as this increases your grade of cleanliness and hence your appeal. Calendar link: http://www.createtheone.com/vedictime (Choose "Actions of a common nature" as the action type)

> The opportunity you have received,
> with eyes you will perceive.
> If you act, you have achieved.
> If you hesitate, you don't believe.

How to know whether he or she is your soulmate

A common question people ask is, "How do I know whether or not they are my soulmate?" Other than the guidance of dreams, here are some ideas:

- Ask yourself, do you want the same things? Is he or she as capable as you? The ancient book of Philip says, "…every act of sexual intercourse which has occurred between those unlike one another is adultery." Orage said, "The only type of sexual relations possible are those with someone who is as advanced and capable as oneself. In either case there will be no feeling of responsibility in regard to progress in the work to interfere. Such a feeling of responsibility should not cut across a sexual relationship. Real sex is impossible if it does. We are not permitted to entertain ideas of development or reform for another person." Some people say they share your interests but when it comes to action there is a resistance. Believe what they do and not what they say. You should not have to change them or convince them. Thoughts of converting them will only get in the way of you loving them. Goethe said, "A marriage can only be called unsuitable when there is a confusion of types, when one of the parties is unable to participate in the manner of existence that is native, habitual, and that becomes increasingly and absolutely necessary to the other."

- Friedrich Nietzsche said, "When entering a marriage one should ask oneself the following question: do you think you will enjoy talking with this woman right up into old age? Everything else in marriage is transitory, for most of your time will be spent in conversation."
- "Judge the love by its works," said Eliphas Levi, "if it elevates the soul, it will inspire devotion and heroic actions; if it is only jealous of the perfection and happiness of the beloved, if it is capable of sacrificing itself for the honor and peace of the beloved, it is an immortal and sublime sentiment; but if it breaks the courage, irritates the will, lowers the aspirations and ignores duty, it is a deadly passion…"
- Ask yourself, "How would I feel if I had to raise a child

with this person?" Imagine it. If nothing inside you disagrees with this image, then they may complement you.

- The wisest woman I ever met told me that a girl must be at least 16 years of age to start a serious relationship with a man.
- Your soulmate is the person who your Intuition wants you to marry. It is a marriage in accordance with the Law of Destiny.
- In the beginning, you or your soulmate may feel an inner resistance towards getting together. There may be fears and all sorts of sensations that arise within you to stop you from uniting with your soulmate. I have dumped one of my soulmates because of these feelings and I have known many women and even another man who have decided to leave their soulmate because of this phenomenon. The key is to not believe every emotion that arises within.
- Here are three ways to know a person quickly: find out what their attitude to sex is, and their attitude to money. And see how they react to adversities. An old man once told me, "If you want to get to know someone, take a big trip with them. In the adverse circumstances that arise during a somewhat unplanned foreign vacation, a person manifests themselves as they truly are."
- You may consider yourself pure and be surprised to find yourself in the presence of a person whose past is filled with sex, drugs and alcohol. Although you may not take drugs yourself, it may be that your soulmate does, or

did. I made the mistake of shunning such people and forgetting the role that karma plays in the soulmate you attract. Therefore do not be so dismissive of partners whose pasts are dark. These circumstances are usually brought about because of your own dark past, even if it was left behind many years ago. "For a long time I searched for a wife, I searched but I found only whores," said Goethe. "In the end I picked you up, little whore, and found a wife." For the women I will rephrase the quote like this (and in some cases I have seen this to be true): "For a long time I looked for a husband, I looked but I found only insecure men. In the end I decided to give the insecure man a chance, and behold I found a husband!" Therefore my word of advice is to overlook where someone has been and look to where they want to go. What the surface exhibits does not always reflect the potential inside.

- With regard to selecting a partner, perhaps the most confronting question you could ask yourself is this: would you give your last drop of blood for this person?
- Women must be careful not to choose a man for mere appearance, or because of the desire to marry, to avoid being alone. When a woman wants to turn a man into her 'ideal', without feeling the truth, psychologically, something won't fit. Many single ladies decide upon the artificial aspects, the form, the financial splendor of one man or another. They try to ingratiate themselves with him in one way or another, to be attractive, they try to accommodate themselves to a way of being or

living – this is not the path of a happy marriage. In real love, there is absolute spontaneity; no type of artifice exists. When a woman instantly recognizes the creative being in a man, then there is no need for superficial words, nor of struggles to adapt themselves to a form of thinking or feeling. In real love, the woman knows if the man complements her or not, if he is hers or not. But when a woman looks at a man and in some way wants something from him, when she knows that there is a characteristic in him that does not coincide with her naturalness, with her personality, or with her psyche, when she believes that she loves a man, and yet feels that there is something which does not belong to her, something like a characteristic trait which in some way she accommodates by her feeling, then that man does not belong to her. Single ladies need to seriously reflect upon what it takes to select the right man, and they need to know how to wait.

- For me, dream-guidance is the surest way of knowing whether or not I should continue dating someone. Dreams, if they are not influenced by the mind, show me the inevitable consequences, they show me the future. Numbers are my second resort. If the number 22 continues to appear before and after contact, e.g. I look at the time and it says 10:22, or 3:22, etc. I know that I am on the way to success. Hermes once said, "God speaks to man in dreams by night and in signs by day." My personal philosophy is a little different: God will guide you through dreams, numbers and intuition.

GRATITUDE

THE CONSCIOUS LAW OF SUCCESS

"You will not get a beautiful lover until you learn to love and appreciate the unfortunate."

— MARKUS ROTHKRANZ, 'SPEECH OF A LIFETIME', 2015

After so many soulmates lost and found and then lost again, I wonder whether it was my lack of conscious gratitude that was to blame. Don't we lose what we don't appreciate? Gratitude, according to self-made billionaire John Templeton, is even the secret to wealth, and 'America's Favorite Entertainer' Steve Harvey said, "Here's the trick to successful people that they never share. The more you are grateful for, the more you say thank you, the more stuff He gives you to be grateful for. That's the trick."

After meeting your soulmate, start thanking the Infinite for it, or the Cosmos, or God, or whatever harmonizes with your understanding. If you don't thank God for the fortunate, the fortune will decrease. If you don't thank God for the unfortunate, the misfortune will increase. Therefore thank the Highest even in loneliness, because as every stick has two ends so too does every suffering have an advantage.

Gratitude is a type of radiant matter given to the invisible world. The response is that the way forward is revealed. Oftentimes we are just one brilliant idea or opportunity away from a breakthrough and feeling gratitude is one way of achieving this. Another aspect is that if the goodness that we have stops satisfying us, if we stop enjoying it, if we stop appreciating it, it goes away. So let's thank God for the goodness that we have and for the suffering that keeps us alert, so that the good increases and the suffering decreases.

Mother Nature makes us pay fines if we do not thank her for the her goods. So let's practice conscious thankfulness to relieve ourselves of the unnecessary suffering that the fines would bring.

I once thanked Nature for the free accommodation I had and a few hours later an even better accommodation was offered to me for free on another continent. The path forward had revealed itself.

Consider whether you want to practice gratitude in your morning prayers or whether you want to feel it spontaneously for seconds here and there throughout the day. Explore it and find your own individual approach to it. And if you don't care to awaken this magical sensation, at least enjoy the good that comes to you as much as you can, letting it deeply satisfy your soul.

Part Three

Courtship

*"There's many a slip
between the cup and the lip."*

– Ancient Proverb

Meeting your soulmate does not guarantee that you will get married. There is still more to know.

In Mozart's 22nd and final opera The Magic Flute, the prince meets his soulmate, Pamina, but there are tests that he needs to pass in order for the final union to take place. The advice that is given to him is: be steadfast, be patient and keep silent.

Pamina is also tested, but differently. She is advised not to believe in a certain assumption she has made about him. Women tend to assume things about men and jump to conclusions too easily. Women need to be aware of this weakness and try to see the truth, they need to strive to see the reality of the man they are dating.

A woman once told me that she almost rejected the man she ended up marrying because of his feminine hands. Her friends convinced her to overlook this detail and continue dating. There is another story of a woman who would continuously reject a certain man's invitations. Fortunately, this man was persistent and eventually this woman accepted his invitation just to shut him up. Well, now they are married. This man knew the value of perseverance and knew that in some cases a woman needs to be approached several times before she agrees. The first rejection is rarely the honest one.

Women oftentimes fall into assumption, men into temptation.

> Angels are known by being loved,
> men are loved by being known.
> You will learn more about each other on a date,
> than in a hundred conversations on the phone.
>
> .

CONTROL YOUR TONGUE

MOZART'S FIRST TEST

*"It is in renouncing the object of lust
that one deserves to possess
the object of true love."*

— ELIPHAS LEVI, THE HISTORY OF MAGIC, 1859

Don't be surprised if you find yourself tempted by another member of the opposite sex even after meeting your soulmate. Every path has its secret tests to evaluate your level of sincerity. In The Magic Flute, the hero must pass three tests before he is granted his soulmate. The first of these is that he must not solicit other members of the opposite sex. The scene portrays charming women using seductive tactics to make him speak but he remains silent and passes. Know that an opera is an artificial way of sharing knowledge with us, which is why we call it art, and the knowledge that this scene is trying to share with us could be elaborated as follows: if, after meeting your soulmate, you greet or solicit the opposite sex with supplication in your heart, you will not see your soulmate for nine days. This is exactly what happened to me. This implies that whenever you talk to sexy people, you have to be careful not to put any sense of flirtation into your words. In the opera the hero knew that in flirting with other women he would be exhibiting poor concentration and dispersing the power of faith. By pursuing multiple women he would catch none. Now let me share with you my own experience of this principle.

On one particular occasion I remember meeting a spiritual photographer on the beach who seemed perfect for me. We talked and arranged to meet at a party that night. After she left I walked to catch a bus and noticed an even more attractive girl at the bus stop provoking me to talk to her. She was a model. I took the bait, talked to her and consequently never again saw the photographer.

On many other occasions I had women approach me and greet me, and I would remain silent. At times I would even appear rude but that is how I passed the test in this particular phase of my life. Now, before moving on, I am not suggesting that the only way to deny the affection of another is to be rude to them. Be courteous. Be gracious. Smile even. My problem is that I used to have the bad habit of talking to every girl I was attracted to so I had to consciously replace this habit with a certain discretion. Now I think before opening my mouth.

I know a lot of guys who cannot stop talking to women. Each and every day, whenever they see a pretty girl, they approach. It is an addiction and they need to let this obsession go if they want to demonstrate loyalty to one woman. My advice: As soon as you meet someone who you believe to be your soulmate, stop flirting with other attractive members of the opposite sex. Instead greet them with a gesture or a smile, but don't open your mouth unless you trust that you can speak without intent. This is easier said than done. It implies that you will somehow know if you meet the right person when you do. I, for example, have met my soulmate without knowing that she was my soulmate. Therefore I encourage you to learn how to distinguish your soulmate from the pack. If you are lucky like me, there will be an unmistakable chemistry or flavor to the encounter. But I suggest you talk things out in the first encounter so that you know then and there whether or not you want the same things in life, or are drawn to the same interests. In short, have a decent conversation the first time you meet someone new to establish whether or not this person even qualifies as your soulmate.

On this topic my last suggestion, something for you to explore, is that after meeting your soulmate, don't even make eye contact with other attractive people. Eye contact exchanges magnetism and sometimes their magnetism will work against you. Wear sunglasses or take control of your gaze. The man who lets himself be caught by the eyes of all women, and the girl who glances into the soul of every man, will have to adjust to changes in fortune as things have not gone according to plan.

HIDE YOUR EAGERNESS

MOZART'S SECOND TEST

"Let love enter disguised as friendship."

— OVID, THE ART OF LOVE, BOOK ONE, 2 AD

As the second test of Mozart's opera approaches, the hero is told to keep silent before his soulmate. When the two of them finally meet, she is glad to see him but he refuses to talk to her. She wonders why he is not talking and gets frustrated with him, begging him to talk. Even so the man remains silent and passes the test.

To keep silent does not mean to literally say nothing, it simply means to hide oneself. Hiding oneself implies that we exercise a certain discretion by hiding information that may startle another. In the context of courtship, it simply means that you hide your neediness, your eagerness, your lust, so as not to frighten them. This principle can be found in the following words of Eliphas Levi: "The sacred love, the virginal love, the love stronger than the tomb, seeks only devotion, and flees frantically before the selfishness of desire." In short, true love begins as friendship.

When I was ignorant of this principle, I would try to kiss my soulmate on the first date. This was a big mistake. Lust makes others feel like you want to take something from them or use them for selfish purposes. You like them, they know you like them, you don't need to tell them. But you must still be affectionate. To show no affection whatsoever would be to go to the other extreme. The middle way is best. You can't walk by using only one foot. By revealing your desire or any hint of possessiveness, your soulmate will go running, as Eliphas Levi pointed out.

In the womb it takes nine months for a baby to grow. No one can speed up that process. It is the same with a soulmate relationship. It grows slowly. It takes time. By trying to speed it up you are challenging a natural law. The kiss is the first step to a sexual relationship and it should not be rushed. However much you desire someone, don't prematurely expose yourself to rejection by revealing your desire until the relationship reaches a certain stage. Actually, relationships progress according to the laws of Venus, in that it takes 240 days for relationships to reach full bloom, because it takes Venus 240 days to complete one rotation.

A know-all 21 year-old friend of mine once told me that she had a boyfriend and that she felt they were soulmates. I became instantly suspicious because the soulmate patterns I had observed did not match her description of the relationship. She told me that she felt a strong connection, that she felt a deep admiration for him, and that she even felt that they were together in a past life. She felt many things. I asked her, "Why do you assume that your feelings are telling you the truth?" She dismissed the question. Within a month the relationship was over. She was a victim of seduction. The belief that passionate relationships begin passionately is simply false. Even the successful marriage of billionaire Tony Robbins began as a friendship.

One day a woman told me about a relationship she had that impressed her deeply. It was the most magical one she had ever experienced. She even moved in with him. Unfortunately it only lasted a week as the dashing prince was having a new girl move in. This so-called prince would pursuade a different girl to move in with him every week. Don't fall prey to the charisma of evil.

Here is a message for all women: don't get into a relationship just because you feel things. You can feel things with anyone! In a real relationship there needs to be a reason to be together. You should have intentions to do things together, not just feel things together. Feeling good now does not mean you will feel good later.

And here is my message for the inexperienced men: when you meet your soulmate, try to want her company in the same way that you want the company of a friend, don't crave her, and if you do desire her, hide it, and don't try to kiss her on the first date. Start the relationship as friends, but be an attractive friend, not the ordinary companion you are to your male friends. Women tend to do this instinctively via three methods: playfulness, compliments and touch.

Ladies, not every man who amazes you is "The One".

Not everything that shines is gold.

Guys, not every woman that blazes with beauty is for you. Not everything that burns is love.

Soulmate relationships do not always start in the bedroom because they have a sincere interest in getting to know each other first. In some cases the woman senses an urgency and is willing to advance the relationship rather quickly. This is rare but it can happen. Most soulmate couples start as friends, friends who are attracted to each other, but in some cases the woman will desire sex quickly. If you like someone who is trying to advance the relationship rather quickly, reassure them that you do indeed like them but would like to get to know them better before starting a serious relationship. Don't offend them. Be considerate. As a general rule though, they kiss not on their first encounter but on their fourth.

Protect Your Creation

Mozart's Third Test

*"Wherever you love or are being loved,
there lie the greatest riches, but there
too lie the world's greatest visible and
invisible thieves the likes of which you
have not even dreamed."*

— Beinsa Douno, Tuning of the Human Soul, V. 1

During the third test of Mozart's Magic Flute, the woman decides to commit suicide because she assumes her soulmate no longer loves her. As she is about to do so, three angels intervene, telling her not to and that she is still wanted by the man she loves. When I first saw this scene I did not understand it. Who was being tested? The man or the woman? What did the suicidal intent mean? And why were there three angels and not one, or four for that matter? What was Mozart trying to tell us? I had to fail this test a number of times before finally figuring it out.

The first clue to deciphering Mozart's third test came after I met one of my soulmates on a particular New Year's Eve. It was obvious that we were perfect for each other. She even reminded me of the soulmate I had waiting in another country. Regardless, she misinterpreted something I said and got upset with me. So she left. Days after I intended to pursue her but I had a prophetic dream that stopped me: I dreamt that she would return home and die.

My second clue was also connected to a dream. As I communicated with my soulmate from another country, I had a dream that she was dead. Later I dreamt that she would be killed. What use was there in warning me of all these deaths? Why was I having these dreams? What was I supposed to do? This soulmate of mine did indeed die, though not physically, and here is where I started to discover my role as creator and protector. I began to see the karmic connection between their sexual choices and their deaths.

The third and last clue came after I lost one of my soulmates to another man. I dreamt of it happening and saw how ugly it made her. This frustrated me so much that I decided to look for a solution and reach out to some people who may be able to help. In this desperate search I came across the keys I was looking for.

In the 1920s one of Beinsa Douno's students had to travel on horseback from one village to another. It was part of his job as border patrol officer. In that year however there were hungry wolves ambushing people in between the villages. In response to the crisis Beinsa Douno armed the man with a series of mental weapons as he did not want him carrying a rifle. The result was that when the wolves tried to take a bite out of his horse, their muzzles wouldn't open. Instead the wolves just bounced off the horse and eventually left him alone. And on his second trip the pack of wolves appeared friendly. But this amazing story does not exist in isolation.

On several occasions some of Beinsa Douno's students had to go to war. Using the prayers they had memorized they all returned alive. There was even one incident where everyone died except the one armed in this way. All these fascinating experiences provided the keys I was needing. If prayer could protect a man from a pack of wolves, then it could also protect my girl from a wolf in a nightclub.

At this point in the chapter, some of you, especially the women, may be thinking, 'Let her choose whoever she likes. She is old enough to make her own decisions. Don't interfere.' But I don't see it that way at all, and after watching several news reports, I have proof.

We reach a responsible age at 21 but this does not mean they magically begin acting responsibly at midnight on their 21st birthday. The knowledge that we have about life between the age of, say, 5 and 25 is often not very different. We are still attracted to stupid things and instead of seeking divine guidance we throw ourselves at these things. If parents have to protect their children then why shouldn't you protect your soulmate? After all, you created them, right? I have seen so many responsible adults enter relationships they would later regret and wonder why on earth they even bothered, as nothing was gained but much was lost.

One of the pieces of knowledge that is so obviously

missing in most people is the role that karma plays in sexual relationships. Upon sexual penetration, the karmic debt of the other fuses with one's one. Psychologically speaking, their demons now inhabit your universe. Their darkness is now yours to work through. Why be saddled with the burdens of another just for a few hours of pleasure? Why would you cover your soul with the egos of another unless you were guided by Wisdom to do so? Medical doctor Franz Hartmann wrote, "By entering wilfully into a sexual relationship with another being, we become attached to it in our will, and a partaker of its future karma." The esoteric teacher Samael Aun Weor wrote, "When someone has sexual intercourse with a person who has been with another partner or other partners, both then absorb the atomic essences of the other partners and poison themselves with them. This is a very grave problem for those aspirants who are dissolving the ego because then, not only do they have to fight against their own errors and defects, but more over, they have to fight against the errors and defects of those other partners with whom they had sexual intercourse." Metaphysical author of over 150 books Torkom Saraydarian wrote, "One person's karma becomes two people's karma through sexual relations, which can be good or bad. That is why you must have sexual relations with only one partner so that you do not load yourself with the karma and pollution of many others."

People cannot be expected to protect themselves so if we know how, we should do the protecting for them.

If it wasn't for those three angels in Mozart's opera, the

woman would have committed spiritual suicide by giving herself to a man with a heavy karmic load. Now, without further ado, here are two prayers to say for the one you love. Beinsa Douno gave these to soldiers before entering the battlefield:

Cosmic Password

Lord, our God, our blessed Heavenly Father, who gave us life and health to rejoice in you, we beg you:

Send us your Spirit to preserve and protect us from every evil and wicked thought.

Teach us to do your will, to sanctify your Name and to glorify you always.

Illuminate our spirit, enlighten our hearts and our minds, so that we keep your commandments and precepts.

Instill your pure thoughts into us and direct us to serve you with joy.

Bless our lives that we devote to you for the good of our brothers and neighbours.

Help us and assist us to grow in all knowledge and wisdom; to learn from Your Word and to abide in Your Truth.

Guide us in everything we think and do in your Name so that Your Kingdom on Earth succeeds.

Feed our souls with Your Heavenly bread, strengthen us with Your power, so that we succeed in life.

As you give us all Your blessings, add also your Love to be our eternal law. For Yours is the kingdom, and the power, and the glory, forever. Amen.

INCANTATION OF PROTECTION

He who dwells in the shelter of the Highest will abide in the shadow of the Almighty.

Regarding the Lord I will say, "He is my refuge and my fortress, my God—I will rely on him." For he will save you from the trapper's net and from the deadly pestilence. He will cover you with his feathers and you will take refuge under his wings: his Truth is a shield and a palisade.

You will not fear the terror by night; nor the arrow that flies by day; nor the pestilence that walks in darkness; nor the destruction that demolishes at noon. A thousand will fall at your side, and ten thousand to your right, but it will not come near you. Only with your eyes will you look and see the penalty of the wicked.

Because you have made the Lord, my refuge, the Highest, your dwelling; nothing evil will happen to you, neither will any plague come near your home. For he will give his angels command over you to preserve you on all your paths. They will lift you up in their hands, so that you do not strike your foot against a stone. You will tread upon a lion and a python; you will trample down a cub and a dragon.

"Because he has put his love in me, therefore will I rescue him. Because he has known my name, I will keep him safe. He will call upon me and I will listen to him. I will be with him in trouble. I will rescue him and glorify him. I will satisfy him with longevity and I will show him my salvation." Amen.

Say them with feeling, three times if necessary, and at different checkpoints during the day. Imagine your soulmate as you do it and use hand gestures to enhance the power of it.

Now, why three angels? Well, ideally we need three levels of protection: the body, the will and the mind. The second reason is that requests such as these often need to be repeated three times to take effect. In all, you may repeat the incantation 9 times in one day. I have obtained results from one strong emotional request, but you may feel like doing three. Dynamic healer Howard Wills noticed that his prayers need to be repeated 3 to 5 times to take full effect.

Lastly, a weak request, formulated in your own words should from my experience be repeated 70 times. Such personal requests should start with, "My Divine Father I beg you to…" The reason why I implore you to pray in this way is because the Father knows whether or not you should be granted the wish. One way to count to 70 is to use your hand, as you have 14 knuckles and 5 fingers, and 5 multiplied by 14 equals 70.

DON'T BOAST ABOUT HAVING MET

*"A good woman is a hidden treasure;
he who discovers her will do well not
to boast about it."*

— PRINCE DE MARCILLAC, REFLECTIONS, XCVI, 1665

By now you may have guessed that luck happens for a reason. Bad luck happens when our actions oppose our aims. Good luck is when we act in accordance with the laws that govern our objectives.

Mozart's Magic Flute tells us to not let ourselves be tempted to say certain things but to think before we speak.

I once knew a man who met The One and got engaged to her. He then introduced her to his family and relatives. One of his relatives gave her such a hard time that she decided to cancel the wedding and leave him altogether. But what is interesting about this is that it happened four different times! He would then meet another girl who he clicked with, get engaged to her, introduce her to his relatives, and she would then end up leaving him before getting married. He told me that an uncle of his for some reason would always insult his fiancee. I told him to keep his next fiance a secret and to never introduce her to his crazy uncle.

One thing worth mentioning here is this: in the same way that weaklings want to divert or hold back the determined man because they are jealous of his power so too do the unloved attempt to divide soulmates.

Boasting invites humiliation and I do have an interesting true story about this: Once upon a time there was a very experienced horse rider. Mounted on his horse, he said to the people around him, "I have never fallen off a horse in my whole life." The horse then bent down in such a way that he fell off, in front of everyone. Telling others about something good can cause them to subconsciously wish you harm, even if they are your so-called friends. I prefer to err on the side of necessity. Tell only those who need to know.

DON'T GIVE A WRONG IMPRESSION

"Things are not taken for what they are, but for how they appear."

— BALTASAR GRACIAN, ART OF PRUDENCE: 130, 1647

During courtship inexperienced men face a danger that women seem to be exempt from. That danger is to make a bad or wrong impression.

There are people who believe that if you are on a date with your soulmate, nothing can go wrong because you belong to each other, you understand each other. That is simply not true. Having dinner with your soulmate may run smoothly the first time but to say that all encounters will run as smoothly as the first is to invite negligence.

Women tend to act better on dates than men because women are by nature motivated by feelings and not by reason. Dates should be dynamic and natural, oh so natural! All men and women should be adorable, and those who are not will become so by learning to follow through with the heart's impulses and not with the ones of the mind.

I enjoyed going on many dates when I was younger and what I found is that a man has to learn to be himself. A man has to undo years of brainwashing that the television was responsible for. Of all the things I have done, one of the best ways to feel more myself was a six-day fast of crushed garlic and diluted lemon juice. To be yourself, you need to feel yourself, and who knows how many impurities are blocking such a feeling!

Don't play games or try seduction or any of that. Be your courageous, generous, and easygoing self. James Allen, in his Eight Pillars, said something very interesting about this:

> *"Of recent years certain pseudo-mystics have been advertising to sell the secret of 'personal magnetism' for so many dollars, by which they purport to show vain people how they can make themselves attractive to others by certain 'occult' means as though attractiveness can be bought and sold, and put on and off like powder and paint. Nor are people who are anxious to be thought attractive, likely to become so, for their vanity is a barrier to it. The very desire to be thought attractive is, in itself, a deception, and it leads to the practice of numerous deceptions. It infers, too, that such people are conscious of lacking the genuine attractions and graces of character, and are on the look out for a substitute; but there is no substitute for beauty of mind and strength of character. Attractiveness, like genius, is lost by being coveted, and possessed by*

those who are too solid and sincere of character to desire it. There is nothing in human nature – nor talent, nor intellect, nor affection, nor beauty of features that can compare in attractive power with that soundness of mind and wholeness of heart which we call sincerity. There is a perennial charm about a sincere man or woman, and they draw about themselves the best specimens of human nature. There can be no personal charm apart from sincerity."

One day I saw a man protesting in the city. His sign said, 'The truth is sexy.' This is perhaps one way of summarizing the passage above.

A certain teacher once said that women already know everything intuitively. Balzac hinted at a similar truth when he dedicated his Physiology of Marriage to men only, saying that women already know it. I will do the same and say that what I have compiled about courtship is for men only, because women already know it. Actually, some of these guidelines have come from women, and some have come from the amusing men I have met along the way. In the beginning, a man may follow these guidelines deliberately, but in the end, he discards them, because he has learnt to be himself. I hope you find them as entertaining as I did hearing them. Many laughs we had over the outlandish comedy of courtship.

Training Wheels For The Men Whose Minds Have Been So Influenced By The Television That They Have Forgotten How To Be Themselves

<u>Guys</u>

"This is a date, not lunch with your mother. Get in the mood for a date. If you arrive early, you're guaranteed to be punctual and this will also give you time to prepare your mood by exercising in a location nearby."

"Ask the Universe to help you act intelligently throughout the date."

"Everything needs plans, even dates. No plan and you'll look like a puppy whose lost his way. Have at least a rough plan for the date. Start with a coffee and end with some form of activity. If you don't have a plan, you won't be her man. But be flexible. And with activities, be goal-driven, not action-driven."

"Don't prolong the date beyond its 'hour of expiry'. A date is ninety minutes or two hours at best. Only natural men can extend it beyond that."

"This is a crazy world, everyone is late and disorganised. One of you will probably be late so make the meeting point a place where waiting is not tiresome."

<u>Ladies</u>

"Please, guys, don't eat garlic or onion beforehand."
"For me, mouth hygiene is everything. Get an electric toothbrush."
"Have cash not coins."
"I've always found hugs to be more personal than kisses, at least while dating."
"Don't say anything wierd when we arrive. Once, as soon as I arrived, the guy started talking about his mother."
"On the first date you should not want me – you have no reason to want me, you don't even know me."

"Don't do on the inside what you are doing on the outside."
"You don't have to be enthusiastic to be fun."
"You are there to be good company to her, not to want things from her."
"What did you notice? Don't think so much."
"Don't act complicated or play games."
"Don't stare."

"That's way too much information."
"The devil is in the details."
"Avoid talking about sex, races, politics or religion."
"Don't hide things."
"Can we have a conversation and not an interview?"

"Her sudden niceness rang off warning bells."
"Have the courage to express yourself in those moments you normally hesitate. Be unrestrained."

"Don't be inconsiderate, rude or sarcastic and never be selfish."

"Don't boast."

"Don't criticise."

"You must compliment her on the first date because she has to know why you want to see her again."

"Give her space, let her breathe. A ray of sunlight will burn if it shines on the same spot for too long."

"Don't overdo the kissing, the hugging or the touching."

"Don't get angry at her. Everyone makes mistakes."

"Don't appear possessive or jealous. Some women are very sensitive to this so don't give her reason to think you are becoming possessive."

"I laughed at the frigidity of his hands. They were colder than a penguin's doodle."

"Don't be demanding."

"Find a reason to see each other again. Have the second date in mind before the first one comes to an end."

"Don't end the date when you're both sick of each other."

"Don't see her off at her doorstep. For heaven's sake, give the girl some privacy!"

"When a guy calls me from home, I get the impression that he has nothing better to do."

"Your best asset is that you're easygoing."

"Always keep your word. Don't say you'll call me and then

not call me."

"Don't read much. You can't go wrong then."
"She doesn't know that I am her soulmate. She's forgotten. She will remember after we spend enough time together."
"Let her pay for her drink if she wants. Don't impose but don't be stingy either."
"Minimise text messages as they can be easily misinterpreted. Most of the arguments I had in my relationship were because of text messages."
"Just hang out."
"Enjoy."
"If she's taken, trust that she is plotting an escape into your arms."
"Garlic makes you smelly, chocolate makes you silly."
"That girl out of your league is actually for you."
"Go into it with the attitude that you will succeed, enjoying the whole process, never doubting."
"It's the age of the soul that counts, not the age of the body."
"Never take rejection personally because it never is personal."
"Make sure you kiss her when she asks. If she holds your gaze and does not look away while she is talking to you, she is asking, kiss her."
"No woman will ever wholly know you. It is impossible."
"You can attract but don't pursue. If you are pursuing you are not being you."
"Women speak a second language, a higher language. If

you understand this language, communication is much smoother. The direction of her face reveals her desire."

"Fridays and Saturdays are best for shopping. Saturdays are also good for hot tubs and haircuts ;)"

Students have often asked me if in all my reading I have ever stumbled across the key to a woman's heart, and I have always disappointed them because quite frankly, I don't like such a question. Perhaps it has never been printed in books because men would only use it for selfish ends. Nevertheless, I decided to go about finding some kind of an answer just to satisfy people. My strategy was simple: ask someone with a ridiculous amount of experience. So I decided to ask a certain friend of mine whose sex life began at age six or seven, and who had always been in long-term relationships. Here is a snippet of our conversation:

"Rodrigo, I was asked recently about what women want," I told him. "I wanted to ask you because of your background. So what is it, of all things? Do you know what women want most, in relationships and in men?"

"Women want to be amused," he answered.

"Ha," I chuckled, "maybe that's why they live longer than men, you know, joy being so good for you…"

"No," he said. "It is not that women live long, it is that men live short. They tend to do more abusing than amusing."

The conversation got a little serious, which was not my intention, and so we took a moment to pause. Then he smiled and said, "Girls just wanna have fun, guys just wanna have girls."

CONSIDER FOLLOWING (OPTIONAL)

Not everyone lives where you do. In some cases, in order for a person to continue seeing their soulmate, travel is necessary. So when meeting people, do not dismiss foreigners just because they are leaving soon. What counts is love and not so much convenience. If they are leaving then consider following. Of course, you may have to keep in touch over the Internet but listen, do whatever it takes for the connection to stay strong. Guys should pick up their phone and make international calls. Emails will not do on their own. Women have the tendency to assume they are unwanted, causing them to seek approval in the arms of other men. Guys, this problem is overcome by regular phone calls.

Part Four

Commitment

*"What is marriage or what preserves it?
Only the knowledge of hearts,
that is its beginning and its end."*

— PARACELSUS, ORIGINAL QUOTE VERIFIED, *1493-1541*

After spending some time with your soulmate, the relationship will naturally become serious, sexual, and then you may choose to get married. However, no relationship is invincible, and that is why I created this fourth part. I want to help you utilize the protective and collective vibration of nature for the preservation of your relationship. Lovers need to produce intelligent effects by using space consciously. "Everything that works is a beginning, not an end," said Goethe.

Many books about marital conduct give, in my opinion, overly specific advice and codes of behavior. I do not want to create robots that mechanically repeat, "I understand, honey!" every few hours, so I have limited myself to giving general advice on nine principles, knowing well that I may have omitted some information but perhaps your intuition will find the rest.

Before going into the principles, I want to encourage you to choose your wedding date carefully. Choosing a positive date to get married can give the beginning of your relationship an advantage, but don't count on it helping your marriage in times of adversity.

Eliphas Levi said, "The new moon is favorable at the beginning of all magical works." Choose a date between the new moon and the full moon, but not on the new moon itself. Humans are mostly water and the moon controls the waters, so its influence is not superstitious but scientific.

Try to choose positive numbers as dates: 1, 3, 19, 22, 28. December 20th 2011 = 3 + 2 + 4 = 9. In a date, double digits are deduced to a single digit before the three numbers are added. The date itself, as in the 20th, is also of some influence. Try to marry in the following hours: 1, 2, 3, 5, 8, 10, or 11. Friday being the day of Venus may also help. And try to marry when Venus is waxing, that is, between the inferior and superior solar conjunctions, e.g., between 26 Oct 2018 and 14 Aug 2019. Marrying between the winter solstice and the spring equinox would coincide with the movements of the Sun. Jesus was born on the winter solstice, symbolizing the Christic force coming forth when soulmates unite. Now don't turn this science into a paranoia. Intuition is the highest science even in matters of astrology and numerology.

To be fair, I am not a marriage expert, and that is why I looked for a set of principles that couples could follow. I did find them, and here they are, Paramahansa Yogananda's 7 principles for married couples:

1. Refrain from display of a possessive attitude. Avoid intrusion on each other's privacy.
2. Recognize each other's independence.
3. Be chivalrous and kind always.
4. Let the home life be simple and the spiritual life deep. Meditate together.
5. Enjoy simple pleasures in each other's company.
6. Guard the tongue and the actions in all ways.
7. Live a healthful life; the right kind of food is important.

Benjamin Franklin's advice was much simpler: "Before marriage keep your eyes wide open. After keep them half shut."

In summary, if your sex life is great and not depleting you of your vitality, if the two of you continue to exercise and grow from within, if you are anticipating your lover's deepest wishes, if you are introducing intervals and giving each other space, if there is variety and play without arguments or jealousy, if there are no kinks in your domestic duties together, then thank God you have such a wonderful marriage.

VARIETY

"Whoever wants to keep a spouse or a lover, should always leave them something to desire, every day you should promise them something new for tomorrow. Vary their pleasures, secure for them the charm of variety in the same object, and I will vouch for their perseverance and loyalty."

— CHARLES EVREMOND, LETTER TO NINON DE L'ENCLOS, C. 1695

Satiety, that is, getting so much of the same thing that you get sick of it, is often the result of monotony. Try to anticipate monotony, try to sense it before it takes hold. When you get a feeling that things are getting stagnant or boring, change something. Postponing satiety is one of the great secrets of marriage. Of course, this happens naturally in an intelligent couple but in the practical world it is often a matter of conscious variation that makes satiety impossible.

Eliphas Levi once said, "To act always in the same sense and in the same way is to overload one of the scales, and absolute destruction of equilibrium is a rapid result."

Variety in the bedroom, variety in expression, and even variety in the cuisine!

Always be introducing change.

When variety's ignored,
couples get bored.
I told him to change,
he changed and he scored!

Maintain Magnetism

*"Attractiveness is the direct outcome
of simplicity."*

— James Allen, The Eight Pillars of Prosperity, 1911

Eliphas Levi said that when a couple fall in love, the man sees the woman as a fairy, an angel, and the woman sees the man as a hero, almost a god. He says that the optical illusion continues as long as the man plays the role of a hero and the woman that of an angel.

If the woman starts to do things that are not in accordance with her feminine nature, she can become ugly to the man. One such thing is to be loud and snappy. And if the man starts to compete with his wife, or if he starts to get timid or shy, he starts to lose that quality of heroism that she once saw in him. Exceptional role playing is what is needed in both parties, and intelligence will go a long way in ensuring this.

Of course, as mentioned earlier, real magnetism or

attraction comes from how a person feels. Therefore, the husband and wife should also look after themselves on a daily basis, so that they are feeling good, loving and energetic as often as possible. That is not to say that the couple won't ever feel sad or weak. Some states are bound to come at some point. But there are many dark moments which can be avoided simply by taking better care of ourselves.

Exercise and time out for relaxation is always recommended. Too many hours at work or engaging in activities that lower one's inner state are often discouraged. The influences that are likely to be a hindrance to a healthy emotional life are intellectual activities such as excessive reading and negative emotional influences such as violent media or aggressive forms of music. Our health also needs to be looked after so the food, air, and how we perceive the world needs to be carefully considered. Of course, women have to take a certain extra care over their physical looks but that goes without saying.

So, to recap, a couple will remain attractive if they play their roles as hero or angel well, look after their health, and their emotions. Attractiveness over time involves good role playing, a certain feel-good lifestyle, eating well and exercising well. This is part of the path of growth and many people know it and do it by heart but I felt it was necessary to mention it: keep being the brilliant person you were when you met.

Lastly, in married life an effort is sometimes made to look younger. The ones who claim to hold the key to eternal youth are often not particularly young in appearance and if we study what happened to Ninon de l'Enclos, we may discover why. Ninon looked like she was in her 20s even at the old age of 85. Reports say she had a crowd following her wherever she went. There were crowds of men who wanted her sexually and there were crowds of women who wanted her secrets. Eliphas Levi claimed to reveal this secret in the following words: "The great magical means of preserving the youth of the body is to prevent the soul from growing old by preciously preserving that original freshness of feelings and thoughts which the corrupt world calls illusions, and which we will call the primitive mirages of eternal truth." George Adamski's mysterious account said more or less the same thing, that it was due to "an ability to preserve the qualities of mental activity, interest and enthusiasm beyond the average." Peter Kelder's Eye of Revelation was the first account to reveal the rejuvenating exercises of Tibet. It is commonly believed that anyone who did such exercises everyday would never look older than forty. I have found them to work but I have always found meditation to have a stronger effect on myself and others. On one occasion, I remember greeting my mother when she returned from an intensive meditation retreat and I swear, she looked ten years younger! The used key is always bright.

WORK TOGETHER

"Nearly half (48%) of couples who are extremely happy share housework equally, compared to just one-third (33%) of those who aren't so happy."

— THE NORMAL BAR, 2012

A real couple is a team. Husbands and wives should figure out their strengths and their time constraints and work together, making domestic life a breeze.

If domestic organization is carried out well, there should be no confusion, and no forgetfulness or imbalances. If the man does more than the woman, or the woman does more than the man, or if one of them forgets, conflict is bound to arise, so see to it that work in the home is evenly distributed.

Once you have discussed the matter and worked out who is going to do what, consider making adjustments in the future as nothing can stay the same forever.

AVOID ARGUMENTS

"Be gone, quarrels and battles of bitter tongues: love is fed with sweet and tender words."

— OVID, ARS AMATORIA 2.1518, 2 AD

In a lustful relationship, arguments can often fuel the fire. But in the case of love, arguments can only extinguish it.

There is only one person in the world you'll ever wholly get along with and that is yourself. Everyone who is different to you will annoy you at some point, particularly if you live with them. People need to understand one another and respect one another's differences. We need the courage to deal with problems at their beginning and not after their storm. In other words, always finish the argument.

There are books that say that the best way to ensure a lasting marriage is to avoid arguments.

Some people choose to ignore the defects of another, while others run away from conflict. I think it is best to confront each situation with as much awareness as possible in order to capture its inner meaning, thereby understanding its solution. In any case, to criticize someone, or to argue with someone, is almost always out of place because people are rarely to blame as most people do not know any better. Everyone makes mistakes. Mistakes are part of existence. So why point the finger?

It is said that the frustration of a woman during her menstrual period is one of the causes of arguments and that is why, a long time ago, wives would take a seven-day vacation to a special place where there were only women on their cycle. This guaranteed no marital arguments as there were no husbands present. When that tradition stopped, a new one was born, the one where, during their cycle, women would not bathe, due to a negative effect on the energies. I know some women in Europe who did this when they were younger but the tradition has since faded away. They would wash their locals and under their arms but nothing more. Nowadays there are tents in which women gather in order to undergo their menstrual period alone. As far as I know, the The Natural Fertility Community and the Rudolf Steiner school teachers have links to such Red Tent gatherings.

I was once told that one of the other secret causes of arguments is the magnetic direction of the bed. I don't know if there is a best direction for everyone, some say the crown of the head should point east…if you think this may be affecting the way you feel then make adjustments until you find a position that suits you.

Avoiding arguments involves not only detaching oneself from the urge to argue but also removing the causes of frustration. Some couples find that they have to sleep in separate rooms because of the persistent disturbance of snoring and fidgeting, but this is a very individual matter. Snoring, from my experience, can be fixed naturally overnight by putting the barefeet on the earth for 8 hours. An earthing mat can be used to achieve this.

Always leaving the toilet seat down and always sitting down to pee is another simple solution for a common frustration that women have.

Feelings of laziness will often overwhelm the inhabitants of a house that is too big for them. This is because unused rooms infect the rest of the house with their stagnant energy.

Of course, there are many causes of frustration that I could address in this chapter but instead I'll conclude with a poem which may help pacify the state of frustration itself:

A home filled with natural aromas,
music, candlelight and plants,
is not so good for arguments,
but good for removing your pants.

AVOID JEALOUSY

"Suspicion breeds contempt."

— M., THE LORD GOD OF TRUTH WITHIN, 1941

One day a single woman in her fifties told me about the only three serious relationships she ever had. What she said was that it was she who ended all of the relationships and that she ended them for only one reason: the man got jealous. "Every jealousy is a suspicion and every suspicion is an outrage."

Jealousy displays insecurity and insecurity is unattractive. Don't be ugly, you're in a relationship! If you have love, show it. If you have jealousy, don't show it.

Let your lover be. Don't impose your will as it only darkens the situation. People have free will and we must respect it. Being possessive doesn't keep a person because its pressure is uncomfortable and who wants to remain in an uncomfortable position?

One of the traps that men need to avoid is misinterpreting a situation. His wife flirts with the waiter and he goes jumping to all sorts of conclusions. Even if the flirting was real, how would fury solve the problem?

If your partner is trying the affection of another, it may be because they are missing something in the relationship. I knew a single woman who would go out and buy herself flowers. Now what are we to think if she had a boyfriend who would not buy her flowers unless he was told to? Men need to be receptive to a woman's changing needs.

Some women get jealous when their husband shows interest in younger women but this is unnecessary. Women should never forget that men by nature adore totally natural beauty and an innocent smile. A man wants to see in a woman sincerity, simplicity, true unselfish love, and that innocent naive frankness that we see in nature. A mature woman with these attributes is sexier than a young woman without them. For there is beauty not only in the way a woman looks but also in the way she expresses herself.

Give to your lover all things and they won't feel compelled to seek things elsewhere.

> Those who strive always to the utmost,
> it is them who We can save.
> Love is as strong as death,
> jealousy as cruel as the grave.

CONSCIOUS LOVE

*"Constant efforts to anticipate the
emerging wishes of the beloved while
they are still unconscious are the
means to conscious love."*

— ALFRED RICHARD ORAGE, ON LOVE, 1932

Conscious love is the force that preserves and maintains not only a relationship but the entire universe.

The highest way of thinking is not thinking. The highest way of loving is conscious loving.

In married life, and in life in general, people hope to preserve things by doing the bare minimum. No one wants to do more than they need. It is said that Mozart would often leave romantic notes for his wife though there was no need to. Now ask yourself, 'What value is there in doing only what you are told?' A truly good servant exceeds expectations.

There is conscious love in the husband who goes beyond the norm, beyond the necessary to serve his wife, beyond what he has been told to do.

There is conscious love in the wife who makes sacrifices to serve her husband, sacrifices that are prompted not by necessity but by the respect in her own heart.

To love on autopilot, automatically, accidentally, to leave love to chance, to love by impulse and not by choice, to let our habits do the loving for us, is to love on a lower level. Love but without interfering with them.

> "Take hold tightly; let go lightly. This is one of the great secrets of happiness in love."
> – ORAGE

Orage said that to anticipate the emerging wishes of the beloved while those wishes are still unconscious, is the way to conscious love. In this approach there is a sincere effort, one that creates and therefore earns true love. So keep making efforts to predict and provide for your lover's wishes while those wishes are still unconscious. Dr. John Gottmann, one of the most respected marriage experts in the world, makes a reference to this approach in the third principle of his book, claiming that "romance grows" in those moments when we attend to wishes as soon as they become known.

> "If you want to enjoy love purely, keep cockiness and seriousness far from your heart."
> – GOETHE

A psychotherapist once said, "Don't sweat the small stuff." I say, it is better to sweat the small stuff now than to suffer the big stuff later on. But don't misinterpret what I am saying. Sometimes we spend way too much time and energy on the most insignificant things. We must realize that a little thing should not require a big effort. In this sense he was right. Do not make a big issue of the little things, but attend to all things gracefully.

In the pleasure of loving the soul finds its way home. Raise that simple and plain love to the highest summits!

If love brought you together then love will keep you together. Love is fed with love.

Conscious love is the art of love, the art of knowing how to love. If we want to preserve the magic of the honeymoon, then we need to put an end to anger, jealousy and selfish demands. And we need to learn to forgive all the mistakes of our beloved. No one is born perfect.

"It is unselfish love given with no demands which links people together, as married people would find out if they gave each other their freedom, and were honest with each other," said the mystic.

Spouses should know that they each have psychological defects, and that these defects must be forgiven. We don't want reactionary behavior, we need reflection and understanding.

Husbands, if your wife insults you, remain serene and gentle. If your wife cries, kiss her tears or caress her, or wait until the emotion has passed, then love her.

Wives, if your husband insults you, love him all the more, and eventually he will awaken to his mistake and beg for forgiveness.

> "Here is how the issue of marriage is put: the husband expects and wants peace, stillness and exhaustion; the wife dreams about the emotions of beginning, the joys of the soul, the middle of spring, dawn! One wants to sleep, the other awakens."
>
> – VICTOR HUGO

The home is an opportunity to see our errors and remove them. To see an imperfection within our spouse or within ourselves may be difficult at first but if we work at removing these things we can turn the home into a paradise. "Domestic bliss is won at the expense of a hidden battle," said the magician. "The more you respect each other, the closer you will unite.""

PLAY

"Play often evokes love."

— OVID, THE ART OF LOVE, BOOK III, 2 AD

If love is joy itself, then doing fun things together would naturally bring more love into the relationship, right? Throughout your relationship keep play in mind and be creative as to its approach.

SPACE

> *"Let there be spaces in your togetherness. And let the winds of the heavens dance between you."*
>
> — KHALIL GIBRAN, THE PROPHET, 1923

Physicists have observed that if two magnets remain connected without intervals, the power of attraction is eventually lost. This also applies to couples.

On one occasion I found myself in the presence of a certain special husband, one endowed with a great deal of love and understanding. I told him about my keys to marriage and he said that one key was missing: "Spouses should not always eat together, though dinner is usually fine." What surprised me about this was that it correlated precisely with Winston Churchill's experiences. "My wife and I tried two or three times in the last forty years to have breakfast together," he said, "but it didn't work...I don't think our married life would have been nearly so happy if we both had dressed and come down for breakfast after all these years."

Man and woman are the two columns of the temple. These columns should neither be too far apart nor too close together, there should be a space so that the light can pass between them. But how much space exactly? I'm not sure but let us examine this question theoretically: Wise men have observed that Nature has allocated two hours for lovemaking every morning and two hours for rest on Saturdays. Now if God rests for one seventh of the time then he would rest for approximately 3.5 hours in any 24 hour day. Of course, experimentation is required but theoretically, a 2-4 hour daily interval makes the most sense, or one full day a week.

Beinsa Douno said, "If you want to be happy in love, keep a rational distance between you and your lover. If you reduce this distance you will lose the love." And bestselling relationship author Esther Perel said, "Fire needs air. Desire needs space."

Space also applies to thinking about them. To think about them constantly is to crowd their mental space and control them. Wish them well and let them be. The soul wants freedom of expression above all things.

KAREZZA

*"Karezza, or the way of caresses, gives
us the key to a complete affectionate
and sexual happiness."*

— Dr. Arnold Krumm-Heller, Thaumaturgy Course, 1948

Sex is the heart of marriage. If the sex is good, so is the marriage. If the sex is bad, make it good.

Most people think that there is only one way to have sex. In reality there are two, depending on what is done with the sexual energy. The sexual energy either moves outwards to dissipate into the atmosphere, or inwards to accumulate in the heart. There is sex that ends in spasm and there is sex that ends in sublimation.

Spastic sex is what we commonly refer to as conventional sex. Sublime sex is usually called Karezza, which means *caress* in Italian. Both approaches are pleasurable but as we have explained, they do not have the same outcome. I cannot say that one approach is 'better' than the other because it really depends on what you wish to achieve.

Conventional sex is easy, while Karezza tends to be more

difficult. Conventional sex can be done with anyone, while Karezza requires a certain type of partner, one who you truly love. Conventional sex can go on quite mechanically, while Karezza requires a certain conscious participation. The high of conventional sex brings instant lows in men and gradual lows in women, but the highs of Karezza do not bring lows. Karezza slowly develops the inner world, while conventional sex sacrifices this world for the sake of putting more babies in the outer world. Conventional sex is the act of rutting, Karezza an act of will.

Plato said that the urge for orgasm exists to create animals, and he was right, it exists to guarantee the continuation of the species. It is part of Nature's program. But we do not have to remain animals, we can be humans, and happy ones at that.

If you want happiness more than babies, then Karezza would be a convenient choice, however Karezza can also make babies, though differently. If you like making babies and making lust even more than your own inner growth, then conventional sex would be appropriate. My advice to those who choose conventional sex would be to strengthen your love to such an extent that no negativity can touch you.

There is also an *illuminating* variation of Karezza and it has been given different names throughout history. For now I will call it Tantrism and say that it caters for those interested in spirituality, while Karezza is for everyone else. Karezza and Tantrism, which are the two variations of soul sex, agree mainly in the following ways: there are no spasms, no animal passions, but plenty of love and high emotions.

When we combine the observations of Steiner, Gurdjieff, George Adamski, and the Torah, we get the following picture: that thousands of years ago, we were all happy and lived in paradise. Then, for mysterious reasons, people started experimenting with sex and eating the forbidden fruit, engaging in the sexual spasm, and then divisions were born and conflict began. What this means is that sex produces the deepest psychological changes and that all wars and idiocies stem from that. If we expand upon this idea, we draw the following conclusion: the world will only improve if the people improve. The people will only improve if they adopt the more loving approach to sex, and such an approach will only be adopted if people have their soulmates, because for such an intercourse to take place we need a partner who we genuinely love.

> "When we compare ordinary sex with Karezza, we notice that ordinary sex often spends itself in exhaustion and can even be followed by depression. On the other hand, Karezza is followed by exhilaration, a sense of power, and great satisfaction."
> – DR. BERNARD JENSEN

It is interesting to note that Yeshua's first appearance was at a wedding. He said, "When you make the male and female into one...then you will enter the Kingdom." Krishna, the christ of the Hindus, made a complementary statement when he said, "I am sex that does not violate spiritual principles." Manu, who various schools believe to be the progenitor of the current human race, said, "A sexual connection involving semen afflicts a man with inauspiciousness for three days." Mosheh, in the third book of the Torah, is taught, "When a woman has sex with a man, and there is an emission of semen, they shall bathe in water, and be unclean until the night."

Gautama Buddha, many centuries ago, took on the responsibility of teaching India about the path to enlightenment. In those days the Indians spoke Sanskrit and one of his Sanskrit sayings that survived was, "Buddhatvam Yosit yoni samasritam", which means, "Enlightenment is in the sexual organs of a woman." The sage Ramakrishna agreed, saying, "God is in the vagina." Padmasambhava, the teacher who appeared many centuries later and who took on the responsibility of bringing this teaching to Bhutan and Tibet, also said that a woman is necessary to enlightenment. Padmasambhava's wife, Yeshe Tsogyal, has written about her tantric experiences with great delight and there are not many accounts quite like it. As far as I know, Marnia Robinson and Dr. Alice Stockham are the only other women to have written about a higher sexuality. Tsogyal wrote about Tantrism. Robinson and Stockham wrote about Karezza. Dr. Stanley Bass, Dr. Arnold Krumm-Heller, Dr. Bernard Jensen and Alex Allman have also discussed the benefits of Karezza. One of the scientific discoveries that Robinson highlights is that dopamine, a neurochemical required for emotional bonds to stay strong, fluctuates after orgasm. One of the unique discoveries made by Krumm-Heller was that physiologically, a woman needs caresses, not orgasms. He went on to say, "A man can and should gently insert the phallus and keep it inside the female so that a divine sensation happens to both, full of joy that can last whole hours, withdrawing it when orgasm approaches in order to avoid the ejaculation of semen."

The current Dalai Lama, responsible for bringing a very elementary version of the Buddhist teaching to the West, has also given the tantric teaching but only to certain people. As I have pointed out in the first chapter of Part Two, he says that the best opportunity for further development is during sex, and that spilling the semen is a "fault". Some people ask, "Why hasn't the Dalai Lama taught this to the whole world?" Padmasambhava suggests that Tantrism is not fit for skeptics, though I would say that the unwritten rule that is being applied here is: If they don't ask, don't tell. Desire is in the asking: if you don't ask, you won't receive.

For those who wish to know more about the sexual aspect of Buddhism, the Tachikawa Ryu teaching and Yeshe Tsogyal's autobiography are good places to start.

Buddhists, doctors and sages are not the only ones to have revealed the harmful effects of orgasm. Even Shakespeare wrote about it:

"A bliss in proof, and proved, a very woe,

Before, a joy proposed; behind, a dream."

Napoleon Hill, the bestselling author of Think and Grow Rich, also gave a warning: "The major reason why the majority of men who succeed do not begin to do so before the age of forty to fifty, is their tendency to DISSIPATE their energies through over indulgence in physical expression of the emotion of sex. The majority of men never learn that the urge of sex has other possibilities, which far transcend in importance, that of mere physical expression."

This 'dissipation' of the sexual energies is also mentioned

in Lao Tzu's Hua Hu Ching.

Some people say, "But orgasm is natural!" And it is, it is the natural consequence of taking sexual pleasure too far. It is just one example of how the body responds to something excessive. Here are some other examples, formulated in third-person narrative:

He got so overwhelmed with feelings of sadness that he burst into tears; his body temperature rose to such an extent that he fainted; he got so engrossed in thoughts that it caused him a nosebleed; he allowed his frustration to reach such extremes that he exploded with anger; he drank so much alcohol that he started vomiting; he got so carried away with lust that his body started to seize up, and his member started to cry white tears. These are all natural explosions that should never have happened. Sexual pleasure is a natural thing, but if we indulge too much, the body erupts. Pleasure is made for us, but we are not made for it.

Those who are interested in finding out how to practice Karezza should consult a book that deals with the subject in more detail. In this book I will only be providing tips that may not be included in other books:
1. Orgasm must be avoided in both sexes, not just in men. Some men believe that women will not be interested in such an approach, but time will reveal the falsehood of this belief. Actually, according to the Ann Landers survey of 1985, 72 per cent of women prefer cuddling over [conventional] sex.

2. If children are not desired, make a request to your Eternal Mother beforehand so that her force stops accidental conceptions from taking place.
3. If impotence or frigidity is encountered, try using something natural to treat it. Maca, pistachio nuts, sprouted chickpeas and mandrake root have helped a lot of people but there is also passiflora, or passion flower, which is supposed to help treat the frigidity of a woman. A doctor once wrote that after having blessed the passion flower and commanded the soul of the plant to light the erotic fire of his wife, the husband should pull it out of the ground. Then he should rub its leaves between his hands and then embrace his wife's hands with his humid hands. I have no personal experience of this so in order to find a natural substance that works, experiment and search one out for yourselves.
4. With regard to timing, I was told that contrary to certain beliefs, sex during the daytime can still be internally productive.
5. Sex should begin naturally and spontaneously. It should be lucid, not mechanical. A certain amount of intelligence is required in order for its nuances to be perceived. Certain books may appear to encourage a mechanical approach to sex but that is certainly not their intention. The sexual act is not mechanical, but by breaking up the act into a certain number of steps, it unfortunately gives some of us the impression of being mechanical. If I told you that the best way to brush your teeth is by following five steps, by first applying the toothpaste,

then wetting the brush but only slightly, then brushing for three minutes, then rinsing your mouth out, and lastly cleaning your brush, would that make brushing your teeth mechanical? We will discover what is natural by following systems that to some appear mechanical.
6. Karezza can produce children but differently: During sex the couple pray to their Eternal Mother, asking Her to impregnate the woman. If the prayer is heard the divine force will extract one sperm from the man and conception will take place. The children of this type of sex are apparently born with superior qualities. No sex is to be had during pregnancy as well as six months after the baby is born. Sex is begun once the milk in the woman dries up.
7. Sex once a day is supposed to be 'enough' and is the general recommendation.
8. Sex should be avoided during a woman's seven-day menstrual cycle.

Here is a list of just some of Karezza's advantages:
1. The couple grow in beauty, magnetism and youth.
2. It satisfies a woman's need of love and caresses.
3. Sex happens more frequently as the desire does not fade and the energy is not exhausted.
4. The love grows and does not die.
5. It naturally prevents unwanted pregnancies.

A woman I knew had always engaged in conventional sex and she was never successful in maintaining a relationship.

After reading a book about Karezza she became enthusiastic and decided she would try it. Before long, she met a nice man and started doing Karezza with him. She said it was interesting. Time passed and, surprisingly, the relationship was still going. Then one day she said that they had broken up. A friend of mine asked her, "Did you stop doing Karezza?" She replied, snappily, "Oh, it wasn't that! Things got complicated." "So you did go back to orgasm?" asked my friend. "Yes," she replied. This particular woman did not fulfill some of Karezza's requirements, so for her, falling back into conventional sex was inevitable.

A friend of mine once told me about a moment he had after a successful tantric session with his girlfriend. He told me that after the session he walked into another room to look in the mirror. He said, "I could feel this amazing energy shooting throughout my body! I felt so alive, so strong. I looked at the world through the window and thought to myself, 'Oh! You animals have no idea what you're missing – that is not sex, that is what animals do. *This* is sex!'" I was a personal witness to seeing him only minutes after he first did Tantrism and I don't think I have ever witnessed such a magnetic man in my whole life. His atmosphere was pulsating. To women he was irresistible, to men he was captivating, persuasive.

A wealthy businessman once said to me, "I only started paying for prostitutes after getting a girlfriend." He told me that after entering a conventional relationship and engaging in conventional sex, he became even more frustrated than he was before. Why? Because conventional sex feeds sexual frustration by feeding lust. The short-term effects of the spasm for a man include a temporary loss of energy, loss of interest in the woman and even a loss of potency. Long-term effects include frustration and a lack of love in general.

A woman whose many sexual desires led to much misery in life once told me, "First comes the sex, then come the arguments." She had never made love, I don't think she even knew that a more loving approach to sex existed. Researchers are now finding, after all these years, that the spasm has a way of triggering certain subconscious elements and making arguments out of nothing. A famous American comedian once joked, "It doesn't matter how many orgasms I give my wife, she will always find something to argue with me about."

A womanizer once said to me, "After sex all women become nagging." Krumm-Heller said that conventional sex transforms the character of a woman into becoming "irritable", "uncompromising", and that she can even start testing the patience of her husband by "meaningless demands". Many divorcees have openly admitted to me that their divorce was the result of a 'transformation' of which they do not know the cause.

Epilogue

An artist is sitting in the moonlight on the edge of the water. A small boat floats by carrying romance, glory, and the mirages that the memory cries over. Already indifferent to the memory of these things, the daydreaming artist drops his flute and watches them pass by without smiling, doing nothing to retrieve them.

The artist…but no, what am I saying, he is no longer an artist, his soul is pacified and his fingers crippled. He is a man of money who dreams of fortune, he wants to grow old at his worktable. To him, glory and romances are an annoying shadow, he gave them up and no longer knows how to see them.

Ah! To the heart the mirages have no age whatsoever, and middle age is not at all the decline of beautiful days.

Anacreon was a much wiser artist. Wandering from coast to coast, he sang, he always sang, and sustained by romances, he went after that boat swimming.

Springtime is no illusion for the swallows: they have the courage to go after it and they always find it again.

Stay in touch

In order to receive new ideas and to catch hold of them sooner rather than later, connect with me here:
  Web: CreateTheOne.com
  Instagram: createtheone
  Email: support@createtheone.com

Help me help others find love. Spread the word. Let's get this book into the hands of 100 million people. And if you have access to any sources of wisdom that should be included in this book, please contact me. At the moment Belsebuub and Beinsa Douno are my favorite sources. My goal is to make the third edition even more complete than the second, but I can't do it without the help of others.

Notes

My First Instructions

1. Edmond Bordeaux Szekely. 1981. Peace Book 1. [ONLINE] Available at: http://www.essene.com/GospelOfPeace/peace1.html. [Accessed 5 May 2018]. The Jesus excerpt has been modified from the original by the author.
2. The Wisdom of the Zohar: An Anthology of Texts, ed. Isaiah Tishby, trans. David Goldstein, 3 vols. (London: Littman Library of Jewish Civilization, 1989), vol. 3, p. 1382
3. Gurdjieff Internet Guide. 1944. Meetings 1941 - 1944 - Gurdjieff, George Ivanovitch. [ONLINE] Available at: http://www.gurdjieff-internet.com/article_details.php?ID=285&W=19. [Accessed 5 May 2018].
4. Journey with Omraam. 2015. Finding your Soulmate - Journey with Omraam. [ONLINE] Available at: https://with-omraam.com/blog/finding-your-soulmate/. [Accessed 5 May 2018].
5. Yogananda, P., 2004. The Second Coming of Christ: The Resurrection of the Christ Within You. 1st ed. Los Angeles: Self-Realization Fellowship, vol. 2, d. 62, p. 1215
6. The Sacred Hawaiian Way. 2018. Kahuna Hale Makua - TheSacred Hawaiian Way. [ONLINE] Available at: http://www.thesacredhawaiianway.com/kahuna-hale-makua.html. [Accessed 5 May 2018].
7. Wilkerson, C., 1973. Soul-Mates. 1st ed. Pacific Palisades: Cosmic Wisdom Publishers, pp. 81-82
8. Ibid. 7, p. 71

The Six Tablets

1. Rudolf Steiner, *KOSMOGONIE, NEUNTER VORTRAG*, Paris, 2 June 1906 (http://fvn-rs.net/PDF/GA/GA094.pdf), p. 65. Accessed August 9, 2013. Translated from German by author.
2. Arnoldo Krumm-Heller (Huiracocha), Mentalismo (http://eruizf.com/masonico/anexo/r_c/arnold_krumm_heller/arnold_krumm_heller_mentalismo.pdf), p. 10. Accessed August 13, 2013. Translated from Spanish by author.
3. Gregg Braden. See "Our Beliefs Can Change the World" (http://www.youtube.com/watch?v=E6a7PSxyiZA). Accessed August 13, 2013.

4. Rudolf Steiner, SIEBENTER VORTRAG Dornach, 2 August 1924. (http://fvn-rs.net/index.php?option=com_content&view=article&id=3788%3Asiebenter-vortrag-dornach-2-august-1924&catid=252%3Aga-354-die-schoepfung-der-welt-und-des-menschen-er&Itemid=19). Accessed August 13, 2013. Translated from German by author.
5. Wilt Chamberlain, Wilt spoke of regrets, women and Meadowlark. (http://static.espn.go.com/nba/news/1999/1012/110905.html). Accessed August 13, 2013.

Rudolf Steiner full page quote
1. Rudold Steiner, Die Theosophie des Rosenkreuzers, Dreizehnter Vortrag, 1907, (http://anthroposophie.byu.edu/vortraege/099.pdf), p. 150. Accessed August 9, 2013. Translated from German by author.

Environment
1. Churchill, W., 1973. Winston Churchill. Architectural Association Quarterly, 5, 45.
2. Grant Cardone. (2017). Could Moving Be the Best Thing You Ever Did? - Grant Cardone. [Online Video]. 14 November 2017. Available from: https://youtu.be/g5so9il657g. [Accessed: 24 June 2018].

Resignation
1. Original Beethoven quote: Ergebenheit, innigste Ergebenheit in dein Schicksal! Nur diese kann dir die Opfer zu dem Dienstgeschäft geben.

Keep your desire a secret
1. Rumi, J. trans. Nicholson, R. (1926). The Mathnawi of Jalalud'din Rumi: Volume I & II. 1st ed. Cambridge: The Trustees of the "E.J.W. Gibb Memorial", p. 36.

Avoid incompatible company
1. Paramahansa Yogananda, *How To Be A Success* (Nevada City: Crystal Clarity Publishers, 2008), p. 87.
2. Aubrey Marcus. (2017). AMP #103 - Hustle Like You're Ugly with Jamie Foxx | Aubrey Marcus Podcast. [Online Video]. 14 June 2017. Available from: https://www.youtube.com/watch?v=G2Ajq9hM_Ck. [Accessed: 24

June 2018] 25:35.
3. Rumi, J., 2017. trans. Jawid Mojaddedi. *The Masnavi. Book Four.* 1st ed. Oxford: Oxford University Press, p. 9.

Eliminate angry thoughts
1. Dushkova, Zinovia, 2016. *Leaves of Maitreya's Garden: The Call of the Heart (The Teaching of the Heart Book 1)* (Kindle Location 1738). Moscow: Radiant Books. Kindle Edition, Part II, 30 November.

Impeccable behavior
1. Sivananda, S., 2015. *Sure Ways For Success in Life and God Realisation.* 19th ed. Uttarakhand: The Divine Life Society, p. 200
2. The Nazarenes of Mount Carmel. 1981. *Peace Book 1.* [ONLINE] Available at: http://essene.com/GospelOfPeace/peace1.html. [Accessed 24 June 2018]. "Wake not by night, neither sleep by day, lest the angels of God depart from you."
3. Sivananda, S., 2015. *Sure Ways For Success in Life and God Realisation.* 19th ed. Uttarakhand: The Divine Life Society, p. 198
4. Kriyananda, S., 2004. *Conversations with Yogananda.* 1st ed. Nevada City: Crystal Clarity Publishers, #167, p. 198
5. The Nazarenes of Mount Carmel. 1981. *Gospel Of Peace Book Two.* [ONLINE] Available at: http://www.essene.com/GospelOfPeace/peace2.html#BookOfMoses. [Accessed 24 June 2018]. Ten Commandments.

Part Two: Creation
1. Tom Bilyeu. (2018). *How to Get Clarity in Your Life / Rob Dyrdek on Impact Theory.* [Online Video]. 23 January 2018. Available from: https://youtu.be/z1fXr4ORF54?t=46m19s. [Accessed: 24 June 2018].

Chastity
1. Ruhani Satsang USA. 1971. *Light of Kirpal: Ojas: The Power of Chastity.* [ONLINE] Available at: http://www.ruhanisatsangusa.org/lok/ojas.htm. [Accessed 25 June 2018]. Kabir quote.
2. ManTalks. (2016). *Preston Smiles - Intuition, Love and Vulnerability.* [Online Video]. 19 December 2016. Available from: https://youtu.be/HcjuUE0CBEY?t=30m27s. [Accessed: 5 July 2018].

3. Marnia Robinson, Cupid's Poisoned Arrow (Berkeley: North Atlantic Books, 2009).
4. Dalai Lama. A Survey of the Paths of Tibetan Buddhism By His Holiness the Dalai Lama: http://www.lamayeshe.com/index.php?sect=article&id=421. Accessed August 13, 2013.
5. Aristotle, On The Generation of Animals, trans. by Arthur Platt, (http://www.davemckay.co.uk/philosophy/aristotle/aristotle.php?name=on.the.generation.of.animals.platt.01), Book One. Accessed August 13, 2013.
6. Refer to Gurdjieff's Beelzebub's Tales. See http://www.holybooks.com/wp-content/uploads/Beelzebubs-Tales-to-His-Grandson-by-G-I-Gurdjieff.pdf p. 255, Chapter 23. Search 'is almost everywhere called 'exioëhary'.
7. Refer to Gurdjieff's Meetings: www.gurdjieff-internet.com/article_details.php?ID=291&W=19. Search 'unilateral manner'.
8. Dr. Arnoldo Krumm-Heller, Curso de Taumaturgia, VIII. Translated from Spanish by author. http://www.iglisaw.com/docs/libros_espanol/krumm_heller/ktaumaturgia.pdf. Accessed August 13, 2013.
9. Ed. Matt, D., 2018. The Zohar, volume 1. 1st ed. Stanford: Stanford University Press, p. 355
10. Manu, The Laws of Manu. Translated from the Hindu, by Wendy Doniger O'Flaherty & Brian Smith (England: Penguin, 1991), p. 105.
11. Agni Yoga Society. 2016. Leaves of Moryas Garden II (Illumination) | The Teaching of the Living Ethic. [ONLINE] Available at: http://agniyoga.org/ay_en/Leaves-of-Moryas-Garden-II.php. [Accessed 25 June 2018].
12. Moses, Leviticus, 15:16.

Conviction

13. Sivananda, S., 2015. *Sure Ways For Success in Life and God Realisation*. 19th ed. Uttarakhand: The Divine Life Society, p. 44
14. The Passionate Few by Omar Elattar. (2018). *ED MYLETT: Broke To $400 Million! (Must Watch Interview)*. [Online Video]. 17 February 2018. Available from: https://youtu.be/W9gEb_bPQZg?t=40m00s. [Accessed: 25 June 2018].
15. Andrea Dandolo. 2010. *Gurdjieff's Talk on Self- Obseration,New York, December 9, 1930 | Sarmoung's Blog*. [ONLINE] Available at: https://sarmoung.wordpress.com/2010/09/10/gurdjieffs-talk-on-self-obserationnew-york-december-9-1930/. [Accessed 25 June 2018].
16. Tom Bilyeu, April 17 2018. Facebook post. [ONLINE] Available at: https://

www.facebook.com/tombilyeu/photos/a.784391455007819.1073741827.784391411674490/1687042964742659/?type=3&theater [Accessed 25 June 2018].
17. Yukteswar quote: Paramahansa Yogananda, *Man's Eternal Quest* (Los Angeles: The Self-Realization Fellowship, 1982), p. 355.

Consciousness
1. Danaos, K., 2018. *The Magus of Java: Teachings of an Authentic Taoist Immortal*. 1st ed. Rochester: Inner Traditions, p. 97.

Charity
2. Awaken. 2013. *Playboy Interview: Anthony (Tony) Robbins | Awaken*. [ONLINE] Available at: http://www.awaken.com/2013/08/playboy-interview-anthony-tony-robbins/. [Accessed 25 June 2018].
3. chungsoo. 2018. *February 2018 – Secrets of Heaven*. [ONLINE] Available at: https://secrestsofheaven.com/2018/02/. [Accessed 25 June 2018].
4. Todeschi, K., 1999. *Edgar Cayce on Soul Mates*. Virginia Beach: A.R.E. Press, p. 142.
5. Sivananda, S., 2011. *How to Cultivate Virtues and Eradicate Vices*. 11th ed. Uttarakhand: The Divine Life Society, p. 266. "Do charity regularly, every month..."
6. Roach, Geshe M., 2013. *The Karma of Love*. 1st ed. New Jersey: Diamond Cutter Press.
7. Mike Michelsen. 2013. *Interesting facts from "King Gautrek's saga" | Mikes passing thoughts Blog*. [ONLINE] Available at: https://mikespassingthoughts.wordpress.com/2013/09/13/interesting-facts-from-king-gautreks-saga/. [Accessed 25 June 2018]. "Good luck to a generous man!"
8. The Nazarenes of Mount Carmel. 1981. *Peace Book 1*. [ONLINE] Available at: http://essene.com/GospelOfPeace/peace1.html. [Accessed 25 June 2018]. Jesus on fasting.
9. The Nazarenes of Mount Carmel. 2016. *Leaves of Moryas Garden II (Illumination) | The Teaching of the Living Ethic*. [ONLINE] Available at: http://agniyoga.org/ay_en/Leaves-of-Moryas-Garden-II.php. [Accessed 25 June 2018].

Beauty
1. Iyer, Vishwanath. 2013. *Yoga and Love* (Kindle Location 2569). Kindle

Edition, Chapter Nine: Key 5.
2. Sivananda, S., 2015. *Sure Ways For Success in Life and God Realisation.* 19th ed. Uttarakhand: The Divine Life Society, p. 43

Suggestion
3. Gurdjieff Heritage Society. 1950. *Chapter XXXIII – Beelzebub as Professional Hypnotist.* [ONLINE] Available at: https://gurdjieff-heritage-society.org/beelzebub/chapter-xxxiii-beelzebub-as-professional-hypnotist/. [Accessed 25 June 2018].
4. *The Law of Success.* (1928). [ebook] Meriden: The Ralston University Press, p.355. Available at: http://4motivi.com/books/hill/lawofsuccess.pdf [Accessed 25 Jun. 2018]. "The method through which you eliminate procrastination is based upon a well known and scientifically tested principle of psychology which has been referred to in the two preceding lessons of this course as Autosuggestion."
5. Clip King. (2017). PAUL STAMETS TELLS ROGAN THAT HE STOPPED STUTTERING AFTER A HEROIC DOSE OF PSILOCYBIN. [Online Video]. 9 November 2017. Available from: https://youtu.be/3h39ax9iu6o?t=5m3s. [Accessed: 25 June 2018].
6. Linda Kaye. 2007. Keen: Psychiclinda's Sensual Blog : Prosperity Affirmation by Anthony Robbins. [ONLINE] Available at: https://www.keen.com/CommunityServer/UserBlogPosts/psychiclinda/Prosperity-Affirmation-by-Anthony-Robbins/148116.aspx. [Accessed 25 June 2018].
7. iTunes. (2015). The Ziglar Show. 320. [ONLINE]. 31 May 2015. Available from: https://www.ziglar.com/show/show-320-most-life-changing-thing-youll-ever-encounter/ [Accessed: 25 June 2018].
8. Interestingly, by studying people and their 'reference groups' over a 30 year period, Dr David McClelland of Harvard University discovered that 95% of our success or failure is determined by the people we habitually associate with. In high-level sport, most coaches and athletes will readily admit that 50 to 95 percent of success is due to mental factors

Intuition
1. Marsilio Ficino, Three Books on Life (Binghamton: Center for Medieval and Early Renaissance Studies, 1989), pp. 371-373. Quote modernized by author.
2. Kaylee Richards. 2016. *Recommended Reads: Love Does – Live Salted.*

[ONLINE] Available at: http://www.livesalted.com/recommended-reads-love-does/. [Accessed 25 June 2018].

Action
1. Robinson, J. (editor), 1996. *The Nag Hammadi Library in English.* 4th ed. Leiden: E.J. Brill, p. 146 "every act of sexual intercourse ' which has occurred between those unlike ' one another is adultery."

Gratitude
1. Markus Rothkranz. (2016). *SPEECH OF A LIFETIME ! Passionate Words to Live By: Markus Rothkranz.* [Online Video]. 6 September 2016. Available from: https://www.youtube.com/watch?v=GWF576mAnnI. [Accessed: 30 June 2018].
2. GaryVee. (2017). *Tony Robbins, Unshakeable, Gratitude & Focusing on Your Steak | #AskGaryVee 242.* [Online Video]. 1 March 2017. Available from: https://youtu.be/9O8haH2tHWY. [Accessed: 26 June 2018]. Templeton and gratitude.
3. Steve TV Show. (2015). *Steve Harvey Uncut: A Simple Trick to Achieve Success.* [Online Video]. 5 March 2015. Available from: https://www.youtube.com/watch?time_continue=7&v=VI4M3EuKRoc. [Accessed: 30 June 2018].

Protect your creation
1. Saraydarian, T., 1999. *Sex, Family, and the Woman in Society.* 2nd ed. Cave Creek: TSG Publishing Foundation, p. 32

Part Four: Marriage
1. The New Earth. 1956. Inside the Spaceships, Flying Saucers have landed. [ONLINE] Available at: http://www.thenewearth.org/InsideTheSpaceShips.html. [Accessed 26 June 2018]. George Adamski's quote.
2. Northrup, C., Witte, J., Schwartz, P., 2012. *The Normal Bar.* 1st ed. New York: Harmony Books, p. 141
3. John Gottman, *The Seven Principles for Making Marriage Work* (New York: Three Rivers Press, 1999), p. 80.
4. Patrick Belton. 2006. *OxBlog.* [ONLINE] Available at: http://oxblog.blogspot.com/2006/01/churchill-on-virtues-of-napping-this.html. [Accessed 26 June

2018]. Winston Churchill's marital happiness.
5. TED. 2013. *Esther Perel: The secret to desire in a long-term relationship.* [ONLINE] Available at: https://en.tiny.ted.com/talks/esther_perel_the_secret_to_desire_in_a_long_term_relationship. [Accessed 26 June 2018].
6. Dr. Arnoldo Krumm-Heller, *Curso de Taumaturgia,* VIII. Translated from Spanish by author. http://www.iglisaw.com/docs/libros_espanol/krumm_heller/ktaumaturgia.pdf, p. 45 [Accessed 26 June 2018]. "La CAREZZA o sea el sistem a de caricias…"
7. Tzu, L., trans. Brian Walker, 1992. *Hua Hu Ching.* 1st ed. New York: HarperCollins, Chapter Sixty-Nine, p. 88.

Plato end page quote
1. Plato, trans. Robin Waterfield, 1998. *Symposium.* 1st ed. Oxford: Oxford University Press, p. 30

"WE HUMAN BEINGS WILL NEVER ATTAIN HAPPINESS UNLESS WE FIND PERFECT LOVE, UNLESS WE EACH COME ACROSS THE LOVE OF OUR LIVES AND THEREBY RECOVER OUR ORIGINAL NATURE."

– PLATO, SYMPOSIUM 193C, TRANS. BY ROBIN WATERFIELD, 385 BC

www.ingramcontent.com/pod-product-compliance
Lightning Source LLC
Chambersburg PA
CBHW032021230426
43671CB00005B/164